Advance Praise for

A STRING AND A PRAYER
HOW TO MAKE AND USE PRAYER BEADS
by ELEANOR WILEY & MAGGIE OMAN SHANNON

"*A String and a Prayer* is an important little book—
a spiritual history, a primer of prayer forms,
a treasure house of understanding. There is
no one who cannot benefit from this book."
—JOAN CHITTISTER, OSB, author of
Illuminated Life and *In Search of Belief*

"Eleanor Wiley and Maggie Oman Shannon
show us that a fine answer to the question of
how to pray is found in our fingertips. People
throughout the ages have known what many of
us are relearning—the things we touch and
see and finger can bring the unseen near."
—REBECCA LAIRD, editor of
Sacred Journey: The Journal of Fellowship in Prayer

"I wholeheartedly recommend this book to all
who are interested in the subject of prayer."
—RON ROTH, author of
Reclaim Your Spiritual Power

A String and a Prayer

A PLACE TO BEGIN

A String and a Prayer

How to Make and Use Prayer Beads

Eleanor Wiley and
Maggie Oman Shannon

Red Wheel

First published in 2002 by
Red Wheel/Weiser, LLC
665 Third Street, Suite 400
San Francisco, CA 94107
www.redwheelweiser.com

ISBN:978-1-59003-010-3
Library of Congress Cataloging-in-Publication Data
Wiley, Eleanor.
    A string and a prayer : how to make and use prayer
beads / Eleanor Wiley and Maggie Oman Shannon.
        p. cm.
Includes bibiographical references.
    ISBN 1-59003-010-9 (pbk.)
    1. Bead—Religious aspects. 2. Prayer. I. Oman Shannon, Maggie,
1958– II. Title
BL619.B43 W55 2002
291.3'7—dc21

                                                2002005704

"How-to" figures in chapter 3 and cover illustrations by Sylvia Bennett.
Cover and workshop photos by Donna Sall Morgan.
Sacred Wheel illustration by Graham Tattersall.

The authors gratefully acknowledge the following people
for permission to reprint their work:
Coleman Barks for "Only Breath" from *The Essential Rumi*, copyright © 1995
Tami Briggs for her poem on page 117
Jennifer Tattersall for her poem on page 110

Typeset in Requiem
Text design by Joyce C. Weston
Cover design by Laura Shaw Design
Printed in Canada
TCP
10 9 8 7 6

To Colette and all the young people of the Balkans
who think of me as a grandmother—they are
the hope of the world.

—EW

This book is dedicated to my precious friend Molly
Starr—and to all those like her who so lovingly and
freely share their kindness, encouragement,
creativity, and beauty with the world.

—MOS

Contents

List of Figures   xiii

Preface: Starting the Strand   xv

Acknowledgments   xxiii

1. Connecting to the Past: The History of Prayer Beads   3

The Religious Use of Beads   4
    Hinduism ❀ Buddhism ❀ Christianity ❀ Islam ❀ Judaism

The Cultural Use of Beads   10
    Greece and Turkey ❀ Native American ❀ African

2. Creating Personal Meaning: The Symbolism of Prayer Beads   15

Elements of Prayer Beads   15
    Colors ❀ Numbers ❀ Stones ❀ Other Materials ❀ Amulets and Charms ❀ Animal Representations ❀ Shapes

Using Amulets and Patterns 31

Colors and Numbers 34

Shapes 35

3. Hands-on Discovery: How to Make Prayer Beads 39

What You'll Need 40

Before You Get Started 43

Four Basic Forms 44

A "Circle of Prayer" ❀ A Prayer-Bead "Shawl" ❀
A Prayer-Bead Bracelet ❀ A Handheld Prayer Piece

4. Opening the Door to the Divine: How to Use Prayer Beads 67

Your Own Practice 67

Beginning a New Day ❀ Walking in the Present Moment ❀
Grounding Practice ❀ Ending the Day ❀ Gaining Strength from
Your Roots ❀ Special Passages ❀ Battling Addictions ❀
Celebrating Achievements ❀ Honoring Your Dreams

Making Prayer Beads for Others 78

Healing ❀ Leave-Taking ❀ Memorializing a Life ❀
Weddings ❀ Babies ❀ Child-Custody Cases ❀
Those in Need of Housing ❀ Those Who Are Lonely

Making Prayer Beads for Communities 86

Caregivers ◉ Families ◉ Teachers ◉ Women and Children
Around the World ◉ Spiritual Leaders ◉ Animals ◉
Earth and the Environment ◉ Rescue Workers ◉
Political Leaders ◉ Peace ◉ Remembrance

5. Prayers for Contemplation with Beads 103

Resources for Further Exploration 121

List of Figures

Figure 1. Applying end tape   46

Figure 2. Closing a circle   47

Figure 3. Closing a crimp bead   48

Figure 4. Shawl styles   51

Figure 5. Adding crimp beads and finishing intial loop   53

Figure 6. Adding crimp beads and finishing end loop   55

Figure 7. Adding loops   57

Figure 8. Making a prayer-bead bracelet   61

Figure 9. Finishing initial loop   65

Preface: Starting the Strand

The use of prayer beads, like all spiritual practices, taps in to deep mysteries that unfold with time. Just as the act of touching each bead happens in succession, so too is there an inherent progression, or evolution, to one's experience of prayer beads. Both of us—Eleanor and Maggie—have been and continue to be joyfully surprised by what the creation and use of prayer beads offers. Truly they seem to have a life of their own. In this book we share many stories of people whose lives have been changed through prayer beads, beginning with our own.

Eleanor began her life as an artist at age fifty-eight. While working as a speech pathologist in long-term care, Eleanor's friend Betty asked her to make some beaded necklaces for a show in 1994. Instead of saying she couldn't, Eleanor said she didn't know how—a slight twist of language that would change her life. With a little instruction, Eleanor made several necklaces. To her surprise, they sold.

On a trip to Bali soon after that, she found what is known as a "Goddess of Transition" (see photo below), a ritual object made of fossilized ivory with an opal navel. It turned out to be a very important amulet. Since Eleanor knew that she would need to find a new job when she returned home, she wanted that carved goddess to remind her of change, so she incorporated it into a bead necklace. Once in her new office, Eleanor was astonished when her new boss looked at Eleanor's beads and

AMY O'CONNELL

GODDESS OF TRANSITION. *Fossil mastodon with opal, jade, stone, fossil, Alaska coral, and sterling silver.*

said, "I have to have that." Eleanor said she couldn't, but her boss persisted. Finally Eleanor said, "You don't even know how much it costs," to which her boss replied, "I don't care!" Now that made Eleanor stop and think. At dinner with friends, Eleanor told this story and they all promptly asked, "Well, do you want to be an artist? If you want to be an artist, you just put a price on the piece and she writes you a check!" So Eleanor named a price, and her boss paid it.

Her first work as a bead artist had passed through her hands. She could not have foreseen what was to come. Eleanor says now, "It all started with that Goddess of Transition—and how complete the transition was!" A week after selling that piece, Eleanor heard from one of her sisters, with whom she had not spoken for five years. The sister had sad news: she had been diagnosed with cancer.

The call was very brief, leaving Eleanor with all sorts of thoughts and questions about how to deal with this information. A few days later, Eleanor received a brochure in the mail for a "Spirituality and Aging" conference in the city where her sister lived. She knew that exhibitors presented at these conferences because she had attended one before. With her sister's condition compelling her to visit, she decided to register with the conference at the same time and display and sell her beaded necklaces. Thus, her new career was launched.

In the beginning, Eleanor was just making and selling

hand-strung jewelry. But one day, when she was preparing a talk on meditation, she decided to look up the word "bead" and found that it is derived from the Anglo-Saxon *bidden* ("to pray") and *bede* ("prayer"). The necklaces she had been creating evolved into the prayer beads that they had really been all along. Eleanor began a new life as an artist, making the decision that she would only show her beads at conferences where she can also talk about prayer, meditation, and present-moment practice.

Prayer beads are so meaningful to Eleanor because they ground us in the present moment, enabling total absorption into the here and now. She also relishes the inevitable surprise when she finishes making a piece, for she never knows beforehand what it will look like. Like our experiences of life, events—and beads—don't always turn out as we plan. For Eleanor, making prayer beads serves as both a meditation practice and a gift.

More than that, she's awed by how prayer beads have opened doors in her life, sometimes literally. Taxi drivers, sales clerks, people in the streets have stopped to inquire about the prayer beads Eleanor wears, creating openings for spontaneous conversations about spirituality. "The beads help us to cut through the superficial and get right down to the most personal and meaningful aspects of our lives," says Eleanor. "And the beads transcend religions, which is what makes them so exciting." For Eleanor, her prayer beads have served as stepping-stones, leading her from a career she'd practiced for thirty years to an unforeseen arena of international travel, artistic expression, and spiritual communion—at an age when most people contemplate retirement.

In July 1998 Eleanor was working as an exhibitor at an Institute of Noetic Sciences (IONS) conference in Kansas City when she met Maggie, who was working as the director of marketing for IONS. The previous year, Maggie had published a collection of prayers from different faith traditions called *Prayers for Healing*. Having this deep interest in prayer herself—as well as a long-held love for the myriad colors and forms of beads—Maggie was immediately captivated by Eleanor's work. Both living in the San Francisco Bay Area, they struck up a friendship.

Maggie was so inspired by her conversations with Eleanor and the possibilities of prayer beads that she incorporated them into a fortieth-birthday celebration with an intimate circle of women. She asked each guest to bring a bead for a necklace that she would use as her prayer beads. She was incredibly moved by the variety of beads, and the sentiments behind them, that the women brought: a clay bead marked with the rune for friendship on it; a tiny aqua glass bell to remind Maggie "to always make noise"; an exquisite face of a wise man carved on a peach pit that had been on a friend's altar; a set of hematite beads to remind Maggie to keep her life in balance. Each bead was so different and evocative that Maggie marveled at the power of a

AMY O'CONNELL

MAGGIE'S 40TH BIRTHDAY NECKLACE

strand with such powerfully symbolic components (see photo above).

"I am very interested in how we can remain spiritually identified in a material world," says Maggie. "At the same time, I love to honor the Mystery by creating something in a visual or tangible form. I was making collages and assemblages around sacred themes, but I couldn't carry them with me. Making prayer beads is a way to create a portable altar."

Since then, Maggie has made prayer beads as a meditation and as a celebration, incorporating elements from her past as well as searching while traveling for new beads. She has given prayer beads to friends in need of healing and has made them for herself as reminders of particular insights that she wants to keep close.

Maggie's interest in beads began in high school. When reading *Slaughterhouse Five,* she was captivated by the thought of beads as a metaphor when author Kurt Vonnegut compared the moments of life to beads on a string. For Maggie, the metaphor has expanded. They are reminders not just of everyday experience, but of the experience of the Divine.

Prayer beads teach us that, because our whole lives are a prayer, there is no need to "go somewhere" to pray. Because we can wear them, carry them, touch them as we drive a car or attend a meeting, prayer beads help us stay close to Spirit in everyday life. The sacred is inside each of us—we need only to call it forth. The physicality of the beads reminds us of spiritual presence, and offers us a tangible way to bring the Intangible near.

We need not invoke the name of God in order to pray. Nor is it necessary to attach any particular spiritual or religious connotation to the beads. Prayer is personal, and the beads are a device for building meaningful ritual into our lives. By infusing prayer beads with personal associations, we can keep our spirituality fresh. We make an ancient practice new and relevant to our contemporary life by creating practices designed to bring us into the present moment.

It is very important to practice our prayer-bead use before we are stressed, fearful, or desperate for grounding. If you develop a good prayer practice when you're calm, you'll be much better able to take yourself to a tranquil place when you do experience stress. In other words, if we do not pray in times of peace, we will have no reference point in times of need.

Throughout this book, we offer many suggestions for different ways that the beads can be made and used, and explore the creative roles they can play in our relationships, ceremonies, and rituals. We encourage you, while making and using your own prayer beads, to seek new kinds of engagement with the present to bring meditation and contemplation into your world. We know that you, like us, will find the beads taking you in directions you never anticipated when you first encounter them. Our prayer and intention is that you will discover interesting practices that resonate deeply within your own life. May the prayer beads be stepping-stones for you as they have been for us. May they open doors to deeper dialogue with others and with the Divine. May you experience the miracles of healing and inspiration that can occur when you begin simply, with a string and a prayer.

Acknowledgments

I would like to acknowledge the following people: Ellen Elizabeth Pillsbury, who asked me to make my first necklace. Shirley Graham, who bought the first piece. Tom Grady, my literary agent, who knew I would write this book before I did. Nancy Levin, who got me started. Maggie Oman Shannon, who collaborated with me on the writing of this book—I couldn't have done it without her.

I have been supported by my family, Jennifer and Geoff; Stewart and Elizabeth; and Graham Tattersall, who did the carving of the Sacred Wheel of Peace. Thanks also to Anne Russell and Dick Verrow for their loving support; the women who literally help me walk through this life: Sylvia, Judy, Vicky, Nancy, Valarie, and Donna Morgan; and the young women who knew I could do it, Maryellen and Laurie.

Thanks to my spiritual advisor Barbara Rose Billings, my spiritual communities of Hesed and Redwood Dharma Center, and all the wonderful teachers of the spiritual traditions of this world; and to all of the people who have shared their stories with me about prayer, present-moment practice, and meditation. I am grateful to you all.

—EW

First, I would like to thank my coauthor, Eleanor Wiley, whose exceptional work with prayer beads and willingness to step into the unforeseen flow of life have been such an inspiration to me. I would also like to thank our agent, Tom Grady; and Jan Johnson and everyone at Red Wheel/Weiser.

Many thanks also go to the people who shared their stories with us. It is a great and moving joy to learn how others have endured the painful passages of their lives with such dignity, courage, and creativity.

Personally, I would like to thank my husband, Scott Shannon; my mother and brother, Jane Oman and Carl Oman; my teacher and mentor, Angeles Arrien; and my inspiring and supportive circle of women friends, for whom I am so grateful. Above all, I give thanks to our Creator, for the infinite gifts of grace, beauty, and love that bejewel this fragile world.

—MOS

A String and a Prayer

To use beads with a prayer, Indian or Moslem or Christian, is to enflesh the words, make thought tangible.

—MADELEINE L'ENGLE
The Summer of the Great-Grandmother

Connecting to the Past:
The History of Prayer Beads

Making, using, and wearing prayer beads creates a tactile communication, linking our senses to universal prayer energy. The first beads were grooved pebbles, bones, and teeth—made over forty thousand years ago—and had talismanic and symbolic connotations from the beginning. For instance, wearing an animal bone or tooth affirmed success in the hunt for food. Beads at this time also served as status symbols. Later in the evolution of human civilization, beads were used as currency. A fossilized shell and bone necklace that is thirty thousand years old, on display at a museum in the Czech Republic, demonstrates that earliest humankind used beads for some of the same reasons people still use them today—for personal adornment, which distinguished oneself from others through unique ornamentation.

Spiritual associations began with the ancient Egyptians, whose use of beads goes back to 3200 B.C. Calling beads *sha sha* strongly implies the beads' talismanic significance, since "sha" is the Egyptian word for luck. Beads officially sanctioned as instruments of prayer have been an important fixture of most spiritual traditions for centuries. And most of the world's inhabitants—nearly two-thirds of the planet's population—pray with beads. Some scholars have theorized that counting prayers naturally evolved from the abacus, the Chinese counting instrument that also uses beads. Others have noted that records of the third-century Desert Mothers and Fathers indicate that they carried in their pockets a specified number of pebbles, which they dropped one by one on the ground as they said each of their prayers.

The Religious Use of Beads

Traditionally, prayer beads have consisted of strings of similarly sized beads, seeds, knots, or even rose petals and beads made from crushed roses, from which we get the word "rosary." The Sanskrit term *japa-mala* means "muttering chaplet," which refers to prayer beads' function as a means of recording the number of prayers muttered. Since counting prayers was initially so important, each religion embracing the use of prayer beads developed its own symbolic structure to follow.

In addition to helping keep one's place in structured

prayers, prayer beads also symbolize the commitment to spiritual life. With their circular form, a string represents the interconnectedness of all who pray. Each bead counted is an individual prayer or mantra, and the rote repetition of prayers and mantras is meant to facilitate a sole focus on the prayer or mantra itself.

✸ *Hinduism*

Most scholars believe that the use of prayer beads originated in ancient India with the Hindus. In India, sandstone representations dating from 185 B.C. show people holding prayer beads, and this practice apparently became widespread by the eighth century B.C. The strand of Hindu prayer beads, called a mala, was designed for wear around the neck, and consisted of 108 beads for repeating mantras or counting one's breath, a practice later adopted by Buddhists. (The word *mala* means "rose" or "garland" in Sanskrit.) The earliest known mala—strung from seeds that still exist—is around two thousand years old.

The 108 beads represented the cosmos, in which people multiplied the sum of the twelve astrological signs by the nine planets. Hindu malas are usually made of natural materials. Beads made from *rudraksha* seeds (called "Shiva's eyes") are used by those in the Hindu cult of Shiva, while devotees of Vishnu usually use beads made from the *tulsi* (sacred basil) plant.

❋ Buddhism

Around 500 B.C., India saw the birth of Buddhism, which adopted the Hindu practice of using a mala for repeating mantras or counting breaths. As Buddhism spread to Tibet, China, and Japan, so did mala use. Like the Hindu mala, Buddhist malas are usually composed of 108 beads—or divisions of that number, fifty-four or twenty-seven beads. While Burmese Buddhist monks prefer strings of black lacquered beads, malas also are made of sandalwood, seeds, stones, or inlaid animal bone. Twenty-seven-bead smaller wrist malas were created to prevent the prayer beads from touching the ground during prostrations.

In Tibet, malas of inlaid bone originally included the skeleton parts of holy men, to remind their users to live lives worthy of the next level of enlightenment. Today's bone malas are made of yak bone, which is sometimes inlaid with turquoise and coral. Buddhists also used their prayer beads as divination tools as well as for prayer.

The 108 beads represent the number of worldly desires or negative emotions that must be overcome before attaining nirvana. Buddhists believe that saying a prayer for each fleshly failing will purify the supplicant.

✳ *Christianity*

Christian prayer beads, most recognizable as the Catholic rosary, are usually made of colored glass or plastic beads, or sometimes beads crafted of olive wood. Although, as noted earlier, there are roots to the prayer practices of the Desert Mothers and Fathers in the third century, prayer-bead use was more widely developed in the sixth century. Then, Saint Benedict of Nursia asked his disciples to pray the 150 Psalms of the Bible at least once a week. Since this was a large assignment for the memory, a substitution of 150 *Paters* ("Our Fathers") was allowed. The faithful used beads to count the *paters*, and this string of 150 beads became known as a *paternoster*. It might surprise some who associate Lady Godiva only with unusual horsemanship, but the first recorded mention of Christian prayer beads occurs in her will. She bequeathed her *paternoster* beads of precious gemstones to the convent she founded in 1057.

The person widely believed to have introduced prayer beads as Christians know them today is Saint Dominic, after he had a visitation by the Blessed Virgin Mary. And Thomas of Contimpre first called them a rosary, from the word *rosarium* or "rose garden," since the faithful used strung rose petals and beads made of crushed rose petals to count prayers. When using a rosary—which is divided into groups of ten beads, called decades—in traditional practice, a Catholic repeats the "Our Father" and "Hail Mary" prayers as he or she marks off the beads with the fingers while meditating on the life of Jesus and Mary.

In the Eastern Orthodox tradition, both knots and beads are used. Shorter knotted ropes are worn on the wrist. Often made of wool, the Greek prayer ropes—called *kombologion*—have thirty-three, fifty, or one hundred knots. Russian *chotki* have thirty-three, one hundred, or five hundred knots. Sometimes the faithful use bead strands resembling a ladder (each end of a bead touching two parallel strands), which signifies the soul making its ascent to heaven.

Christian prayer beads probably once had relationships to the folklore surrounding stones and talismans. Coral, for example, was thought to guard against illness, so in many portraits of Jesus Christ as a child, he is depicted with coral beads. Later, as a result of such associations, clergy were not allowed to use rosaries with beads made of amber, quartz, or coral.

Christian prayer beads have been associated primarily with Roman Catholicism or with the Greek and Russian Orthodox tradition, because John Calvin discouraged their use by Protestant believers. He rejected materialism and ritual, feeling that the faithful should read and analyze spiritual texts in direct relationship with God, rather than simply memorize set prayers.

However, in the late 1980s, an Episcopalian priest created an Anglican rosary of thirty-three beads, which represent the years of Jesus' earthly life. There's also a nondenominational variation known as the "Earth Rosary." Consisting of four sets of thirteen beads, which indicate the thirteen weeks in each of the four seasons, the Earth Rosary has a total of fifty-two beads, representing each week of the year.

Like their secular counterpart "worry beads," prayer beads offer a kinesthetic comfort—they are a means in the material world to remember one's place in the spiritual world. As M. Basil Pennington reminds us in *Praying by Hand: Rediscovering the Rosary as a Way of Prayer,* prayer beads simply are a method or instrument "to help us pray, to enter into communion and union with God. Therefore, we should feel free to use it or pray it in any way that helps us to enter into that union" (33).

✹ Islam

Prayer beads are also used by Muslims. No one knows exactly when or how prayer beads entered this faith tradition, although scholars believe that prayer-bead use in Islam was adopted from Buddhism. Muslims use strings of thirty-three or ninety-nine beads with one "leader" bead, which represent the ninety-nine names of Allah found in the Koran and the one essential name. Called *masbaha* or *subha*—from the Arabic word meaning "to praise"—Muslim prayer beads include markers after the thirty-third and sixty-sixth beads. Often *subha* are made of wood, or from date pits produced in the Islamic holy city of Mecca.

✷ *Judaism*

In Judaism, prayer beads have been considered a form of paganism. However, because the Jewish prayer shawl known as the *tallit* includes a specified number of knots, we can perhaps intuit that numbers are as spiritually significant to the tallit in Judaism as they are to prayer beads in other traditions.

Made of blue and white silk and featuring fringe, five knots, and four tassels, the tallit indicates obedience to a passage in Numbers 15:37—41. In it, Moses asks that the tallit be made and looked at, specifically noting the number of tassels to include "so you will remember all the commands of the Lord."

The Cultural Use of Beads

✷ *Greece and Turkey*

Worry beads, the secular counterpart of prayer beads, are found in the Middle East, Turkey, and Greece, and are also known by their Greek name *komboloi*. Inspired by Islamic prayer beads, *komboloi* usually consist of thirty-three beads (any variation from this will still be an odd number, along with a leader bead). Some have even hypothesized that worry beads evolved as a way of mocking people using a rosary or *subha*. Though they have no specific religious significance, countless people use them to calm and rebalance themselves.

✿ Native American

Beads have always had spiritual significance to Native Americans; neck medallions as early as A.D. 800 served as talismans against threat. Certain items of jewelry and other ornamentation using beads were often integral to their healing ceremonies. For instance, Native Americans first used seashells and quills for their beadwork. Europeans introduced glass beads, which Native people incorporated into their beautiful and colorful work. These tiny beads were called "little spirit seeds" by some tribes, who felt that they were a gift from the gods.

Vestiges of Christian missionaries appear in the rosaries of the Yaqui tribe of Arizona, who have been Christians since the early 1600s. Their culture blends the symbolism of Christianity with their traditional Native beliefs.

Native Americans bring a spiritual philosophy to their beadwork, believing that the time it takes to make items beautiful honors the spirit world. In *A Primer: The Art of Native American Beadwork,* author Z. Susanne Aikman, who is of Eastern

Cherokee descent, counsels using a "Spirit bead," or a bead that stands apart from the rest of the pattern, when creating beads of one's own: "Each piece should contain an intentional mistake or Spirit bead," she writes. "The reason for this is that we are but human and cannot achieve perfection; if we attempt perfection in a piece it could be bad luck. So always remember your Spirit bead" (3).

✹ African

African cultures have long prized beads, though their earliest use served as indicators of power and wealth. Africans also used beads to communicate. The "love letters" of the Zulu tribe manipulate the colors and patterns of beaded offerings to one's suitor in order to convey secret messages. In Rhodesia, Matabele chiefs gave beads to witch doctors as a tribute to their god. These beads were known as "ambassador beads," since they were used to elicit the goodwill of the Divine. For the Yoruba, beads represent the qualities of spiritual wisdom, the power of the gods, and the gods themselves. The Yoruba believe that using beads in ritual or on ritual objects will enhance their power. Diviners wear special bead necklaces that identify them as spiritual leaders and enhance their power. The Masai find beads so meaningful to their culture that their language includes more than forty words for different kinds of beadwork.

Given both the religious and cultural significance that beads have held around the world, we can trust this precedent and explore the spiritual power of beads in our own lives. As we move into the next sections, we invite you to think about creating your own prayer beads as something to do in addition to, not instead of, any current practice you may have.

I have learned that there can be a whole universe in one bead. Colors, textures, and relationships between beads can tell a lifetime of memories. They are spiritual.

—NAN, USA

Creating Personal Meaning:
The Symbolism of Prayer Beads

P rayer beads invite reverence. When making prayer beads of our own, consciously chosen colors, numerical patterns, stones, elements, amulets, and shapes offer powerful personal reminders and meanings. When we take the time to tailor each string to our own particular spiritual situations, our prayer practice can deepen and expand. While the spectrum of such possible personalization is as large as your imagination, here are some ideas to consider as you work.

Elements of Prayer Beads

✤ Colors

Whether or not you subscribe to any of the traditional, religious, cultural, or folkloric associations made to different colors, you no doubt are attracted more to certain colors than others.

Pay attention to your natural leanings. The colors that attract you will be more healing, comforting, and inspiring to you, no matter what the guide below says. As with every aspect of creating your own strand of prayer beads, the elements that "speak" to you are responding to the promptings of your soul. Listen to those impulses—and honor them.

Here's a general guide to cultural associations with certain colors:

White. White symbolizes purity, which is why it is the traditional color for most Western weddings. It also represents initiation, and we see it frequently in rituals marking significant life passages. It is the color of the absolute, and of knowledge and pure light.

Yellow. Resembling the color of the sun, yellow also represents light (and enlightenment); wisdom; harvest (as in the color of grain); and communication. In the Hindu system of mapping energy centers known as *chakras*—Sanskrit for "wheels" or "disks"—yellow is associated with the third chakra, which represents the will, intellect, action, and vitality. The color of the precious metal gold, yellow represents yang (masculine) energy.

Orange. Orange is the color of happiness. Its energy stimulates the appetite and facilitates socializing, which is why so many restaurants are decorated in orange hues. It is also associated with the second chakra, representing sexuality and creativity.

Pink. The soft shades of pink represent love, including love of self.

Red. The stimulating tones of red activate energies, as red also represents fire and blood. This color suggests passion, power, life, and strength. Red is the color associated with the first or root chakra.

Purple. The color purple was originally derived from the dye of a shellfish known as porphyra. Since it was so expensive to manufacture, the color became associated with royalty and with clergy. Perhaps because of these associations, purple also represents the sacred. Among the chakras, it is associated with the seventh or "crown" chakra, which governs understanding, transcendence, and enlightenment. Accordingly, purple is the color of power, honor, and intuition.

Green. The soothing tones of green represent balancing and healing energies. It is a color of hope, growth, and rebirth, and because it appears so often in nature (and in American banknotes), it also suggests abundance. Green is associated with the fourth chakra, known as the "heart" chakra—and thus also represents love.

Blue. The color of the sky and sea, blue especially invites relaxation and meditation. Its cool hues soothe the spirit. Some believe blue also has protective powers. Associated with the sixth chakra, blue or indigo represents imagination, visualization, and clairvoyance. Blue also signifies Divine truth.

Brown. Another color found in nature, brown represents the earth, dirt, and autumn—the cycle of life. In the late Middle Ages, brown also suggested the erotic in lyrical songs and poetry.

Gray. As it blends black and white, gray represents the middle way. Its inherently balanced nature associates readily with mediation; gray is the color that represents justice.

Black. The darkness of black suggests introspection; it symbolizes night, death, and ultimate Mystery. Like the color white, it can represent the absolute. In China, it is considered the color of yin (feminine) energy.

❀ Numbers

Using numbers mindfully when creating prayer beads can also intensify meaning. As we have seen in the previous section, all religions that employ counting prayer beads use a set number of beads to represent particular theological considerations—the 150 psalms, as with the Christian rosary; or the ninety-nine names of Allah, as with Muslim prayer beads. Knowing something about what particular numbers represent in different cultures can add even more meaning to your prayer piece as you count your beads onto their string.

One. A single bead can symbolize the sun, a seed, or the Divine spark. It can also symbolize God, individuality, or oneness with life. In some cultures, it also represents courage.

Two. Two beads together can represent anything that involves relationship, such as marriage or motherhood. It also can symbolize cooperation—the balance of yin and yang, for example—and the moon, which waxes and wanes.

Three. Three is a powerful number, representing manifestation. A triangle has three sides, and, as a sturdy trinity, represents the sacred. It can be a symbol of wholeness (mind-body-spirit), completion (beginning-middle-end), creativity, and joy.

Four. Four is the number of sides of a square, so it represents solidity, will, and discipline. It also represents the earth, and is the number for several important symbols of wholeness, such as the four directions, the four elements, the four stages of life (childhood, youth, adulthood, old age), the four seasons, and the four Evangelists.

Five. Five numbers the points of a star, and as a result suggests both the star and its corresponding shape, the head, two arms, and two legs of a human being. It also can refer to the five senses, or to the five fingers on each hand. It is a number of learning, communication, and freedom.

Six. Six is a healing number, and is considered the number both of creation (as God created the earth in six days) and of perfection. It also symbolizes beauty, pregnancy, and responsibility. In China, 6 is associated with the influences of heaven.

Seven. Seven is a sacred number, considered the most spiritual. It is the number of perfect order and completion. The world was completed in seven days; there are seven energy chakras. It is a number that signifies inner wisdom and spiritual strength.

Eight. Eight signifies strength and energy and authority. It also represents abundance. There are eight trigrams in the I Ching, and turned on its side, the numeral 8 becomes the symbol for infinity.

Nine. Nine generally represents completeness and the end of a cycle. It is also a number that signifies action and service; there are nine Muses who represent the full spectrum of creative accomplishment.

Ten. The number 10 represents accomplishment, as in something that has been completed and perfected. It is a number of transformation and totality: There were Ten Commandments; humans have ten fingers and toes.

Eleven. Eleven represents a higher level of understanding, intuition, and metaphysical abilities. It is also the number of new beginnings, as it follows the completion number of 10.

Twelve. Twelve, as it is the number of signs found in the zodiac, is the number of cosmic order and perfection. Christ had twelve disciples; there are twelve months in a year.

If working with numbers in your prayer beads interests you, you might want to do additional reading in the area of numerology to find out what particular numbers represent in that science. Pay attention, too, to numbers of personal significance, such as ages, birth dates, or anniversary dates. As with every ingredient of prayer beads, what makes their creation significant is what has significance to you.

Stones

There has been a lot of interest in what stones "mean." Those power bracelets of hematite, rose quartz, turquoise, and other single-stone beads so popular in the late nineties got a lot of attention because each kind of stone promised the wearer something specific, such as relief from depression, a better love life, and good health, respectively. Again, their meaning to you is all that's important, whether it's the stone's symbolic properties, its color, or just its shape and feel. For those who are curious, here's a quick rundown of some popular stones made into beads, and what each is associated with in ancient and modern folklore.

Amber. In China, amber was considered to be the soul of a tiger, so it could both enhance one's courage and serve as protective energy. Some use it for balance; others think it's congealed light. Amber is also said to promote magnetism.

Amethyst. Considered a gem of healing, amethyst signifies gentleness, humility, peace of mind, and piety. Considered a remedy for poison and inebriation, it's a good stone to wear for sobriety and against addictions. Amethyst is said to control passion and quicken the intellect. It is also considered a stone of atonement.

Bloodstone. Bloodstone promotes understanding and peace; it is considered the granter of all wishes. Bloodstone is believed to be a healing and transforming stone and is used to calm oneself and create harmony in one's surroundings.

Garnet. The ruby tones of the garnet earned it its name, which derives from the word for pomegranate. Because of this relationship, garnets are associated with the womb, with blood, and with the feminine. Garnets also represent devotion, energy, loyalty, and grace. In Central America, the garnet symbolizes the soul. Garnets are believed to bring prosperity and good fortune.

Hematite. Hematite is so highly regarded as a protector that Roman soldiers used to rub their bodies with powdered hematite before going into battle. It is considered an agent for reducing stress and depression and can deflect negative energy. It is a stone that represents rebirth.

Jade. Jade symbolizes virtue and excellence. Thought to represent the eternal, jade often adorned burial vestments in order to ensure immortality. It is the stone of energy—associated with yang (masculine) power. Jade also symbolizes beauty, clarity, and perfection.

Pearl. A symbol of perfection, the pearl is associated with the feminine principle and the moon. Pearls symbolize chastity and purity; they also represent compassion and spiritual knowledge. Associated with water because of where they are found, pearls can also represent the transformation of pain into beauty (deriving as they are from a grain of sand within an oyster, which then secretes the material that enfolds the irritant and eventually turns it into a pearl). The ancient Greeks considered pearls a symbol of love.

Rose Quartz. Known as the "love stone," rose quartz symbolizes all forms of love, from self-love to romance. It promotes kindness and compassion, and is said to decrease stress and to enhance one's appreciation of beauty.

Tiger's Eye. Like the fierce animal that lends the stone its name, the tiger's eye represents courage, confidence, and energy. It is believed to be a stone of protection. Its light-catching stripes make it a representative of light and dark, as well as of change and growth. Tiger's eye is also associated with creativity. His Holiness the Dalai Lama has worn a mala made of tiger's eye.

Turquoise. Considered sacred by Native Americans, turquoise is a healing and balancing stone that also serves as protection. It is said to amplify courage and to help bring forward one's voice. It is a stone that symbolizes fulfillment and success.

✹ *Other Materials*

Bone. Bone is often used for Buddhist malas; both animal and human bone remind the user of impermanence. Using beads made from animal bone can also invoke the spirit or spiritual qualities of that particular animal.

Clay. Using beads made of clay can add a "grounding" component to one's prayer beads, as clay comes from the earth. Because of this origin, clay represents life itself, as well as the feminine.

Feathers. As they come to us from birds, feathers are associated with the wind, sky, and sun. They may also represent heaven and faith.

Glass. Because of the transparent nature of glass, glass beads can symbolize clarity and light.

Gold or silver. Metal beads have different associations according to the type of metal used; gold generally represents the sun, and silver, the moon.

Knots. Egyptians considered knots symbols of immortality, and Muslims consider knots protective. In Buddhism, the endless knot is an important symbol of longevity and good luck. Knots can be used as a symbol of anything we are bonded to, such as a marriage.

Mirrors. Because they reflect our image back to us, mirrored beads suggest self-knowledge and consciousness. They represent clarity and truth; they reveal to us Divine intelligence and the soul within.

Nuts. Nuts can symbolize humanity; the kernel or sweetmeat inside represents our soul. Beads are sometimes carved out of nuts, though often nuts are used unembellished. In India, the sacred *rudraksha* nut is sold cheaply so that everyone can afford to include it in personal prayer beads.

Seeds. Seeds represent life and the abundance of possibilities for that life, including the possibility of rebirth. Many malas are made out of bodhi seeds, because the Buddha is said to have attained enlightenment under a bodhi tree. In Africa and South America, beads are also made out of coffee beans.

Shells. Shells represent the life force and the feminine, since some shells resemble female genitalia. Cowrie shells in particular make connections to feminine energies.

Wood. Wood, one of the five Chinese elements, represents spring. Wood symbolizes matter, energy, the sacred cycles of life, and Mother Earth. Many malas are made out of sandalwood, a fragrant material with a scent believed to inspire compassion and spiritual insight. And many Christian rosaries are made from olive wood hailing from Jerusalem.

✺ *Amulets and Charms*

Though we sometimes use the words "charm" and "amulet" interchangeably, charms are simply metal depictions of symbols that have significance to you, while amulets may or may not be representations of actual things and could be made of an organic material such as shell or stone.

Although it is not necessary to add amulets or charms to your prayer beads—except for the cross found on the Christian rosary, amulets are not included on the prayer beads of most religious traditions—small pieces can help you focus your prayers. Counting pieces such as a large "guru" bead or marker are usually included in traditional prayer beads; your amulets or charms can serve the same function (or new ones, of significance to you). The important thing is to make your prayer-bead piece something that integrates easily into your life. Sometimes Tibetans will even attach personal items such as keys to their malas—what better symbol of everyday integration could there be?

Here are some charms and their common meanings. See if any of them might nourish your prayer focus.

Anchor. In Christian symbology, the anchor represents hope, fidelity, and steadfastness.

Arrow. Both Hinduism and Buddhism consider the sacred sound "OM" an arrow that pierces ignorance and helps one to reach enlightenment. Arrows also "point the way" to the next steps on our path.

Bell. Bells protect against evil spirits and call us to prayer. As such, they represent the connection between heaven and earth.

Egg. An obvious fertility symbol, the egg also represents possibilities, perfection, life, and resurrection.

Key. In Japan, key charms are a symbol of good luck; in other cultures, they represent access to the Mystery—the tool that unlocks the door to spiritual realms and the treasure within.

Leaves. In Asian countries, leaves represent happiness and well-being. They also symbolize the cycles of life and of nature, of renewal and hope.

Scarab. Considered sacred in ancient Egypt, the scarab beetle is a symbol of resurrection, wisdom, and power.

✹ Animal Representations

Many beads represent the furred, feathered, and scaled companions with whom we share the planet. You may choose to honor a particular creature in your life with a bead representation, or you can invoke an animal's totemic energy that you would like manifested in your life. Below is a sampler of what different animals symbolize in various cultures.

Bear. The bear, because of its hibernation patterns, is associated with the moon, as well as with reawakening and rebirth. The bear connects with power, protection, and strength, as well as healing.

Bee. In ancient Egypt, bees symbolized the soul, death, rebirth, and love. Because of their capacity to make sweet honey, bees are also a symbol of creativity and wealth.

Bird. Birds mediate between heaven and earth and thus are symbols of fate. They also represent higher consciousness, messages from the spirit world, and Divine power.

Cat. Honored in ancient Egypt as sacred, cats are symbols of the Mystery. Cats also represent individuality, independence, and intelligence.

Dog. A protective symbol, dogs represent fidelity and loyalty.

Fish. Because of where they dwell, fish are associated with water and with fertility and abundance. In Asia they are seen as a symbol of happiness; in Christian circles they symbolize Christ and spiritual nourishment. Fish are also thought to represent strength and endurance.

Horse. Horses are associated with strength, speed, power, and grace; they represent freedom and wisdom. The horse is also seen as a symbol of sexuality and masculinity.

Lizard. As it longs for light, the lizard is seen as a symbol of the soul. It is also associated with the dreamtime, divination, and renewal.

Snake. Its ability to shed its skin makes the snake a symbol of initiation, transformation, and self-renewal. Its association with *kundalini*, or cosmic energy, also makes the snake a symbol of sexuality and creativity.

Turtle. The turtle is seen as a symbol of the universe, of immortality and wisdom. It represents stability, strength, and longevity, as well as fertility.

❋ Shapes

Choosing shapes that either interest you or have symbolic significance to you will also contribute meaning to your prayer beads. Here are some common shapes and their familiar representations:

Circle. The circle represents wholeness and perfection, such as that of heaven. Its perfection also suggests unity.

Crescent. In Islam, the crescent represents opening and victory over death. In other cultures, it is associated with the female, with pregnancy and birth.

Cross. In addition to its well-known use in Christianity, the cross represents the horizontal and vertical intersection of heaven and earth, active and passive energies, or a crossroads in life.

Disk. The disk is a symbol of the sun; in China, it represents heavenly perfection.

Spiral. The spiral represents growth and evolution. Its ascending circles recall cycles of development and creativity. It also is associated with the phases of the moon and thus with fertility.

Square. The square, with its four sides, suggests stability, security, and solidity. It is the symbol of the earth and of order and integration.

Star. The star represents cosmic order, as its place in the heavens might suggest. Stars offer guiding light in darkness, as well as suggest constancy.

Triangle. This powerful shape is thought to symbolize the light of God. The triangle represents not only the Christian Trinity but also other triads, such as maiden-mother-crone, mineral-plant-animal, right speech/right thought/right action. In some cultures, the triangle symbolizes the female and fertility.

Wheel. The wheel, so significant in the Buddhist tradition, symbolizes life. Implying change and movement, the wheel is associated with the process of becoming and with rebirth.

Armed with a few symbols and their meaning, we can now notice how others employ colors, charms, materials, and shapes into their prayer-bead pieces. Following are three very different approaches.

Using Amulets and Patterns

A dentist and a twenty-year student of Buddhism, Holly has made a number of malas to remind her of significant life events or insights. During a vision quest one summer, Holly gathered acorns from the base of the tree near which she camped and strung them into a short strand of prayer beads. When she

AMY O'CONNELL

HOLLY'S WRIST MALA

returned to her office, Holly crafted two tiny bees out of dental gold, whose bellies were engraved with the image of an endless knot (see photo above). For Holly, the elements of this mala related the important spiritual lessons of her vision quest. "The making of this mala was my prayer," Holly says, "to bring into the physical plane the learning from that experience, so that I can remember it."

Synthesizing several symbologies, Holly made another mala to honor the four directions (see page 33). She incorporated the colors associated with each direction in Native American culture, and made prayer beads divided into four color quadrants: red, using antique coral beads; black/brown, using amber and bodhi-seed beads; blue, using green Tibetan and Southwestern turquoise beads; and white, using lotus-seed and bone beads. "As I touch the beads, each quarter is made of a different material, so I can tell when I'm going into a new division. It's like the turning of the year," Holly says. "It's like the mala has a memory. It feels like I've developed a relationship with it; like it has a life of its own."

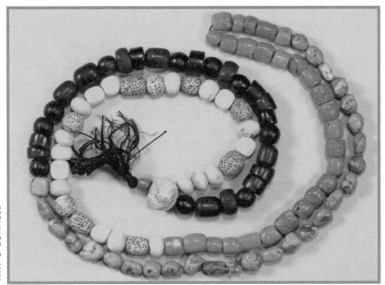

AMY O'CONNELL

HOLLY'S FOUR DIRECTIONS MALA

Colors and Numbers

Anne, an educator in Washington, D.C., has been making prayer beads for years, drawing on the artistic traditions of her African and Native American ancestors. Anne begins her sessions of bead-making by declaring sacred intention, and then follows the inspiration that comes while she works.

Anne believes that the "ingredients" of her prayer beads are powerful parts of the pieces: "The stones and colors have properties. They can help you—serve as allies, supports, guides—if you're conscious about it," she explains. "For instance, I use a lot of amber in my pieces for protection and healing. The energy is there; if you call on it, it's activated. If you don't want it, it's just a beautiful piece of jewelry." When making beads, Anne asks in prayer that the ingredients she uses be charged, so that the energy of their inherent qualities can help people on the spiritual level.

Anne integrates many cosmologies into her work, citing different meanings for various numbers and colors. "The number 5 is very important in African society, and some numbers are universally significant, such as 3, 7, 9, and 11." Colors, too, are chosen purposely. For instance, Anne likes to use red, sometimes adding just a single red bead to a strand: "It's a powerful, protective color; it enlivens, excites, brings vibrant energy. It's something to call on."

The pieces Anne makes for herself help give her "a sense of being grounded and protected and covered." Her advice for people who want to create their own prayer beads? "A person should pray," she says. "They should see what happens; pick up stuff that calls them or particularly attracts them. Whatever it is that resonates with them, there is an ancient tradition behind it that informs that work. It all has underlying meaning—it was never meant to be just pretty."

Shapes

Eleanor created a charm she calls the Sacred Wheel, which has since become a signature piece of her work. She first heard the story of the Sacred Wheel in 1993 from Jim Kenney, the director of the International Interreligious Initiative for the Parliament of the World's Religions in Chicago. Six years later, having launched a livelihood centered on making prayer beads that included symbols of all faith paths, Eleanor decided she needed a symbol that honored all people and creeds. With a friend, Nancy Levin, Eleanor chose the symbols without much research, later discovering that they unconsciously chose archetypal symbols that worked for multiple faith paths. They included the six-pointed star, the cross, the turtle, the OM symbol, the crescent, the five-pointed star, and the spiral. Eleanor chose the words "a place to begin" for the edge of the wheel to serve as a reminder that each moment is a new beginning. After designing the wheel, Eleanor's ex-husband, Graham Tattersall, carved it, readying it to be cast in metal. Now their children delight in this symbol created by their mother and carved by their father.

On the card that accompanies the Sacred Wheel, Eleanor includes these words: "The Sacred Wheel is a mandala of symbols created to honor all spiritual paths. When this medallion is used to bring us into prayer, we embrace the joys and sorrows of all people. The symbols on the outer edge of the wheel are a representation of the rituals we practice, separate from each other; the spokes represent our spiritual path. As we move down the spoke, deeper into our spirituality, we find we come closer together, like the spokes of the wheel. The hub represents emptiness, which allows us to be together in silence."

Eleanor first shared the wheel at the Parliament of the World's Religions in Cape Town, South Africa, bringing it full circle from introduction to manifestation. She conducted a workshop with fifty people from all over the world of all different religions. Together they made personal prayer beads using the wheel as a symbol of unity. Since that time, Eleanor has brought the symbol with her everywhere, including to peace workshops with young people in the Balkans. Little did she dream that those experiences were preparing her for the work that now needs to be done in America.

Eleanor always keeps a wheel or small handheld prayer piece in her pocket so if she encounters someone in need of them, she has them available to give away. When those people tell her that she can't—or shouldn't—do that, Eleanor just smiles and says, "Oh yes, I can; I make them for that purpose. All you have to do is say 'Thank you.'"

For Eleanor, prayer practice with beads—rather than the characteristics of the beads themselves—is what is important. "But," she says, "you have to make your own needs important. A color, a shape, a type of stone might just wake up something in your soul; listen to it, go with it."

Interestingly, even if you eschew the thought of choosing symbols for your prayer beads, your prayer-bead necklace itself is a symbol. According to J. C. Cooper in *An Illustrated Encyclopedia of Traditional Symbols,* the necklace can represent "diversity in unity, the beads or links being the multiplicity of manifestation and the thread and connection the non-manifest; the beads are also men [*sic*], animals and all living things depending on, and being kept together by, the divine power" (111). Whether you agree with Cooper, or see the string as your life and the beads as moments in time, the process of making prayer beads stands as a beautiful metaphor for life itself.

I learned that you should feel when writing, not like Lord Byron on a mountaintop, but like a child stringing beads in kinder-garten—happy, absorbed, and quietly putting one bead on after another.

—BRENDA UELAND
(*If You Want to Write*)

Hands-on Discovery:
How to Make Prayer Beads

When it comes to prayer beads, you are the expert. Your prayer beads are personal and only you know the "right" way to make them. Learning to trust ourselves in the present moment is an important aspect of creating and using contemporary prayer beads. They work as a reminder to bring prayer into our lives—and there is no right way to do that, either. The right way is the way that's right for *you*. As you make your prayer beads, you can develop a present-moment practice of just being with the beads. Allow their structure to evolve and try not to work too hard on deciding how they are going to look.

What follows in this chapter are some basic instructions, beginning with a supply list and various points to consider before starting your prayer beads. These sections lead into four different prayer-bead projects for you to make—a traditional prayer-bead necklace, a prayer-bead "shawl," a bracelet, and a handheld prayer piece.

What You'll Need

Before we begin, here's a list of the supplies you'll need. All materials and tools discussed can be found at your local bead or craft store or ordered from the catalogs and websites listed in the resource section at the end of this book.

- ❖ Bead stringing material—for example, Soft Flex wire or imitation leather thong
- ❖ Crimp beads—used with beading wire to secure the beginning and end of a bead strand
- ❖ Wire cutters
- ❖ Needle-nose pliers—used for bending wire, making repairs, crimping, or doing tight precision work
- ❖ Crimp pliers—used with crimp beads or tubes to make a finished crimp
- ❖ Glue—one that dries fast and clear
- ❖ Bead board—gives you a surface with a narrow necklace-shaped groove in which you can keep your beads steady as you create your design
- ❖ Beads, of course!

You'll find your beads almost anywhere: old necklaces and earrings, thrift stores, boutiques during your travels, bead shops, or places that might surprise you! The potential sources for beads are endless. Amulets and other reminders of your life can be gathered from special events, childhood trinket boxes, souvenir shops during trips, family heirloom collections; they can be stones from the ground or shells from the beach. Every corner of your entire life has potential treasure.

Anything with a hole in it can serve as a bead. In her work, Eleanor has used everything from a cigarette holder to a Balinese rice scoop to a shade pull. Everything can be used, because the practice of mindful creation is more important than the materials. Eleanor got a great lesson on this when she did her first prayer-bead peace workshop in the Balkans. She had asked for bead donations to the project before leaving the United States, and found herself disappointed at the poor quality of some beads, which she considered not bringing. But in reminding herself that each was a genuine gift, she brought every single one of them with her anyway. The response from the young participants was astounding. They were so grateful that people from all over the United States had sent beads for them to use, and whether each was glass, stone, or plastic, all were valuable and beautiful in their eyes.

When you start your project, think about how long you want the piece to last. Every piece will come apart at some time in its life. Knowing this about your new prayer piece will remind you of life's impermanence. Some people deliberately use fragile thread in their prayer beads when they are working on a fragile part of their lives, and keeping watch for frays is one of the practices for that particular kind of creation.

Various materials can be used for stringing beads. Decide for yourself which material is most comfortable for you and which best expresses the metaphors behind the particular piece you're making. One woman, while vacationing at a beach, used dental floss to string shells with holes in them, wanting to use this piece to recall the peace of the rolling waves, the warm sun, and the sand beneath her feet. Dental floss, however, will break quite easily, so unless you consciously want to do a meditation about impermanence, choose something else!

Reliable stringing materials used for making contemporary prayer beads include silk thread and hemp cord (both are used with a beading needle), beading twine, leather cord, elastic cord, and Soft Flex wire. Large pieces are best strung with Soft Flex wire (.019 gauge), which is more expensive than thread or twine but also much stronger, allowing it to accommodate a larger variety of beads and amulets. Beading wire requires the use of crimp beads to secure each end of your piece.

Handheld pieces can be made of hemp cord, leather cord, and even satin cord. Silk thread, hemp cord, beading twine, leather cord, and elastic cord can all be knotted, so no tools are required. Generally speaking, the holes in your beads will need to be larger if you use these stringing materials.

Before You Get Started

Read through all of the following instructions before beginning a piece, so you can decide which steps you want to follow and which seem less important. Steps 1, 2, 3, and 4 may be done in any order. One thing will lead to another.

1. Think about how you want to use the beads. Do you want to wear them as a necklace? Around your wrist? Or just hold them in your hand? Once you have made this decision, you will know how long your stringing material should be.

2. Decide on your stringing material. Small bead holes will require a thin thread like silk or a beading wire like Soft Flex. When using silk, leather, or hemp, you can close your piece using a simple knot instead of a crimp bead. Put a drop of glue on your knot when you're done; this secures the knot and prevents it from loosening. Cut your stringing material four inches longer than the size you want for your finished piece.

3. Choose beads that create visual and textural harmony for you. The number of beads you have collected may be the deciding factor in the size of the piece you decide to make.

4. Find a comfortable, quiet place to work. Place a tray, towel,

or bead board on a table, your lap, or on the floor if you're comfortable working there. The closer you are to the floor, the shorter the distance the beads have to fall when you drop them!

Four Basic Forms

In this section you'll find instructions for four different prayer-bead designs. Always remember that these guidelines are just a place to begin—you do not have to complete your piece as described here. Add or subtract whatever will bring more personal meaning to your piece. What you are making should remind you to bring prayer into your life. As you make this piece, try to find a quiet place and say some simple prayers as you focus on putting the string through each bead.

Whatever approach you take will be the right one for you; the experience is always different for everyone. Allow your own meanings to emerge. In the workshop Eleanor gave for young people in Bulgaria, one of the students wrote: "The beads gave me a new feeling of life. When I string or just touch them, I can fully realize how different we are and that our lifetime is full of various moments—some of them smooth but misleading and others rough but giving a sense of security. Thank you for teaching me how to perceive life!"

CIRCLE OF PRAYER. *A variety of medium-size beads made of glass, clay, bone, and stone.*

✳ A "Circle of Prayer"

The simplest piece is a continuous string of beads. Traditional prayer beads used by Buddhists, Muslims, and Hindus are constructed this way. The piece described will be 36 inches long, strung on Soft Flex wire (.019 gauge).

1. Using the wire cutter, cut a piece of wire 40 inches long and put a small piece of masking or adhesive tape on one end (see figure 1, below). This will keep the beads from falling off when you hold your work out to admire it. You can either string your beads randomly, or plot out a more formal design using the bead board.

2. As you begin to put the string though each bead hole, let your mind rest in the colors and the textures of the beads. Remember that stringing itself is a meditative practice. You can also pray with specific intentions as you add each bead to your strand.

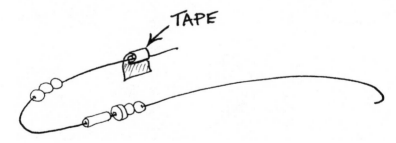

FIGURE 1. APPLYING END TAPE

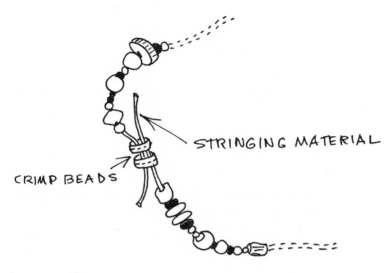

CRIMP BEADS

STRINGING MATERIAL

FIGURE 2. CLOSING A CIRCLE

3. When you have completed 36 inches of beading, you are ready to add your crimp beads. Lay your piece carefully on the table or bead board. Place two crimp beads on the open (untaped) end of your wire. Carefully remove the tape from the other end. Then thread this end of wire back through those same crimp beads (see figure 2, above).

4. Pull each end of your wire so there is a ¼-inch space between your beads and each crimp bead. Take your needle-nose or crimp pliers and squash the crimp beads until they are flat (see figure 3, page 48). This will anchor the beads in place. It takes a little practice to get this right. Practice clos-

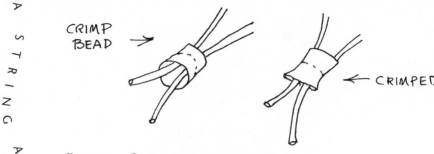

FIGURE 3. CLOSING A CRIMP BEAD

ing a loop with crimp beads a few times before you try completing your prayer piece. Always tug a bit at the closed strand to make sure it is snug.

5. When your piece is secure, trim excess threading material from around the crimp beads.

6. Your piece is ready for use!

A PRAYER-BEAD SHAWL. *Beads included: medallion with ancient writing (pewter), prayer holder, antique hair piece (silver) from India, Wheel of Peace (sterling), snake (pewter), carnelian wrapped with silver, rough crystal, Naga shell, pyrite, small stone (Mali), clay disc (Central America), six-pointed wooden star (Prague), hand-painted Buddha surrounded with silver (India), Hand of God—antique Muslim pendant (Afghanistan). All spacer beads are sterling silver.*

✳ *A Prayer-Bead "Shawl"*

One of the signature formats of Eleanor's work is the "shawl," or open, necklace. As its name suggests, this can be worn like a shawl (see figure 4, page 51); clasped together with a pin or piece of wire; or folded in half, draped around the neck, and "closed" by placing the loose ends through the loop. Eleanor chooses to put several amulets on each end of the pieces she makes—you may choose any number you like for your pieces.

If you want to create a design using matching beads, you first have to decide how long your piece will be and then figure out how many of each bead per inch you'll need to make it. Needless to say, large beads are not as many to an inch as small ones. Beads are generally measured by millimeter: 4mm, eight beads per inch; 6mm, six beads per inch; 8 mm, four beads per inch; 10mm, two to three beads per inch.

Small "seed" beads (the tiny, colorful beads used in the beadwork of many indigenous cultures) are used to make "loops" on the shawl, bracelet, and handheld pieces. They run approximately 16 beads per inch; large seed beads run approximately 12 per inch. Seed beads usually come in plastic vials or small plastic bags—check out the hole size when buying them and make sure you can see their holes.

It's always better to have more beads than not enough—you can keep the extra ones for something else. If you are tall, you may want a long necklace.

FIGURE 4. SHAWL STYLES

1. Decide how long you want your piece to be. The piece described here is 52 inches long as a finished piece so, in this case, you would need to start out with 70 inches of .019 gauge Soft Flex wire. You can use that extra material to make a loop on each end and have something to hold on to while working. Now you are ready to start.

2. To make your initial loop, string on seed beads for about 4 inches—folded, this makes a 2-inch loop on which you can fasten your charms or amulets. Check the amulet you are putting on this loop—is the hole big enough to slide over the seed beads? If not, string half of the seed beads, slip on the amulet, and then add your remaining seed beads. When you have finished stringing what you want on the loop, put on the crimp beads. Plan to use 2 crimp beads for the initial loop and 2 for each loop you wish to add on to the strand later. You can add as many loops as you like, but you need to put *all* the crimp beads on before you make the rest of your piece. It is better to put on too many crimps because you want your piece to be very secure, and once you start the body of your piece, you will not be able to get back to this section—it's now or never!

3. Slide the end of the wire back through the crimp beads. With a pair of needle-nose or crimp pliers, squeeze only the top 2 crimp beads closed (see figure 3, page 48), leaving the others open for your additional loops (see figure 5, page 53). Remember to test the stringing material to make sure it is securely held. You don't want your piece to fall apart.

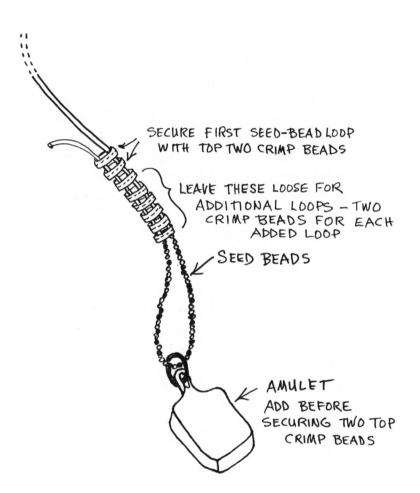

SECURE FIRST SEED-BEAD LOOP
WITH TOP TWO CRIMP BEADS

LEAVE THESE LOOSE FOR
ADDITIONAL LOOPS – TWO
CRIMP BEADS FOR EACH
ADDED LOOP

SEED BEADS

AMULET
ADD BEFORE
SECURING TWO TOP
CRIMP BEADS

FIGURE 5. ADDING CRIMP BEADS AND FINISHING INITIAL LOOP

4. Now you are ready to string the main portion of your piece. Consider using both smooth and rough beads to symbolize the easy and more challenging aspects of life. Once you've picked a standard-sized bead, try this pattern: vary with beads one-third larger, one-third smaller, and then one-third larger again. Practically speaking, smaller (but not tiny) and smoother beads are more comfortable at the back of the neck, but be willing to experiment and even to take your piece apart if you are not satisfied. As you place your beads, pay attention to what calls to you. Ask yourself questions. Listen to yourself. What makes you feel comfortable? What feels scarier, more risky? This is a wonderful time to listen because there are no "right" answers; it is simply a way to get acquainted with yourself. Continue beading for about 48 inches, not counting loops.

5. When you have finished the body of the necklace, it's time to make the loops on the other end. Add the crimp beads *before* making your end loop. Put on 2 crimp beads for your end loop and 2 for each loop you want to add. For example, if you want to add 3 extra loops, string 8 crimp beads on in a row—2 for the end loop, 6 for the extra loops. Now make your end loop by stringing on 4 inches of seed beads, along with your amulet. (NOTE: If your amulet doesn't fit over the beads, see step 2.) Run the end of your wire back through the crimp beads (see figure 6, page 55). *Do not crimp anything at this point.*

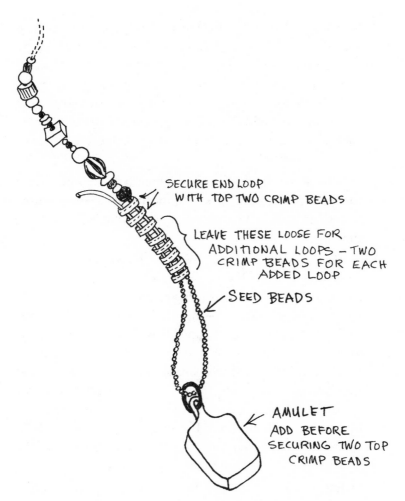

SECURE END LOOP
WITH TOP TWO CRIMP BEADS

LEAVE THESE LOOSE FOR
ADDITIONAL LOOPS — TWO
CRIMP BEADS FOR EACH
ADDED LOOP

SEED BEADS

AMULET
ADD BEFORE
SECURING TWO TOP
CRIMP BEADS

FIGURE 6. ADDING CRIMP BEADS AND FINISHING END LOOP

6. Next, check to be sure that you have no gaps over 1 inch on your string. Pick your piece up very carefully, holding the end securely, and let all the beads slide down to the finished end. You want to leave about 1 inch of wire for working with the loops. Also, you don't want your beads strung too tightly as this could cause your stringing material to break (just as we humans have a tendency to snap if we string ourselves too tightly).

7. When you are satisfied with the length of your piece and the space you have to work with for the loops you are going to add, go ahead and crimp the top 2 crimp beads, leaving the others for your extra loops.

8. It is now time to add the remaining loops to both ends of your piece. Decide how long you want your loop(s), then cut your piece of Soft Flex wire at least 4 inches longer than you need so you have something to hold on to while stringing your loop. Check the amulet you are putting on the loop—is the hole big enough to slide over the seed beads? If not, string half of the seed beads, slip on the amulet, and then add your remaining seed beads. Use smaller beads for the loops when you have several loops at the end of a piece, because they will lie flatter. If you're just including one loop at the bottom of your shawl necklace, then the size of the beads on the loop doesn't matter as much.

9. String your loops and attach each one to the main piece (see figure 7, page 57) using 2 of the crimp beads already on

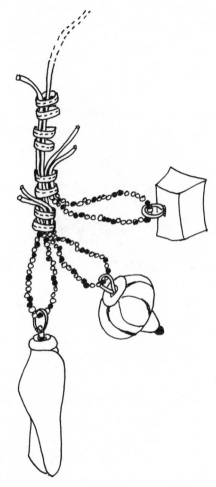

Figure 7. Adding loops

58

WIRE WRAPPING

your bead strand. When you are satisfied with the look of your loop, squash the 2 crimp beads (see figure 3, page 48) and trim off the excess material. Be careful to cut the right string.

10. Once you have added all of your loops to both ends, your piece is finished. If you do not like the look of the exposed crimp or feel that you have too much exposed stringing material, you can buy wire (sterling silver, copper, brass) and wrap it around the parts you don't want to see (see photo above). Sterling-silver wire wrapping is now one of

Eleanor's trademarks. What started out as a means to hide something is now an element that people find particularly pleasing about her work. If you find there is something displeasing about your piece, experiment with wire, ribbon, fabric, or thread as a means of covering and transforming your "mistakes."

A PRAYER-BEAD BRACELET. *Agate, glass, stone, and bone strung on imitation leather with Sacred Wheel of Peace*

✦ A Prayer-Bead Bracelet

Here is a bracelet that you can make with a dangling amulet, so that when you are walking you can hold it in your hand.

See figure 8 below for the following steps.

1. Cut a 20-inch piece of 1.0mm imitation leather thong. (This is available from Fire Mountain. See resources list.)

2. Attach your amulet to the end of your leather thong and secure it with three knots. Put a drop of glue on each of the three knots to hold them together.

3. String beads for about 8 inches or whatever length is right for the size of your wrist.

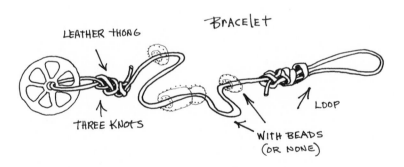

Figure 8. Making a prayer-bead bracelet

4. Now you are ready for your final loop. Make the loop just big enough to slide over your amulet and secure that loop with three knots and a drop of glue. Just slip your amulet through the loop on the other end, then slip it through again, and *Voilá!* You have a bracelet.

HANDHELD PRAYER PIECE: *Beads included: sterling silver Wheel of Peace, pre-Colombian stone bead (Central America), temple beads (Thailand), antique prayer beads (Afghanistan), Kunzite crystal, jade cicada, silk tassel.*

✸ A Handheld Prayer Piece

Handheld prayer beads are not for wearing. While some are small enough to keep in your pocket, larger pieces can hang on the wall or be placed by your bed or on your coffee table. If you display them in a "high traffic" area, they can remind you to take a breath and say a prayer as you pass them.

1. Decide how long you want your piece to be. The one in the photograph on page 63 is 18 inches long with a loop at each end. If your beads are heavy, use .024 Soft Flex wire.

2. Make your initial loop by stringing 2 inches of 4mm beads, your amulet, then 2 more inches of 4mm beads. Add on 2 crimp beads, run the end of your stringing material back through them (see figure 9, page 65) and squeeze them closed to secure the loop.

3. String a variety of beads on your main strand until your piece is as long as you want it to be. Remember to leave at least 4 inches of stringing material at the end for your final loop.

4. When you're done stringing the larger beads, put 2 crimp beads on the stringing material, then add 2 inches of your "loop" beads, your amulet, and then your final 2 inches of beads.

5. Thread your stringing material back through the crimp beads, check to see that you have ¼-inch slack on your stringing material, and crimp your crimp beads flat.

CRIMP TO FINISH

FIGURE 9. FINISHING INITIAL LOOP

6. Test your crimp beads by tugging on your loop.

Again, these directions are only a starting point. You don't have to follow them exactly. Have no expectations of how your piece is going to look when it is finished. Let the beads teach you about yourself and what makes you comfortable.

When we are still, we can perceive things as they are.
When we are still—when the mind is still,
when we are not making things crazy—
there is clarity.

—THICH NHAT HANH

Opening the Door to the Divine: How to Use Prayer Beads

Your Own Practice

By integrating the significant symbols of our life into our prayer beads, we create an adornment that will continually ground us in the present moment, making our entire life sacred. As we've explored earlier in the book, it can be extremely powerful to incorporate beads, talismans, amulets, and other objects from one's own life—as well as diverse spiritual symbols—into our prayer beads to give them deeper meaning.

One man we worked with made prayer beads using a cross that was his father's from World War II, as well as some beads from an old rosary he had as a child. A woman incorporated a rock she had found on the beach that looked like a skull. With a wire wrap around it, she was able to add it to her prayer-bead strand.

As these examples suggest, beads become powerful and metaphoric containers for our experiences in life. Mixing textures (rough and smooth beads together) commemorates the challenging and the easier passages of our experience. Using spacers between the beads can mark the times when we feel there's not much happening. Those times are sacred, too. Similarly, it is important to pay attention to the characteristics that make us who we are—to know ourselves in our fullness—in order to grow comfortable with ourselves. By weaving the elements of our lives into our prayer beads, we can begin to contemplate the multiple meanings of those elements. As we come to understand each separate influence by working our beads, we see how powerfully prayer can change our lives.

One striking illustration of this transformation is the strand of prayer beads that a woman made for her mother to honor the lives of her two dead sisters. Using elements representative of each sister, the daughter made prayer beads for her mother that celebrated her lost daughters' memories. The mother wears them every day, keeping all three of her daughters close to her in prayer.

In making prayer beads, we carry the contemplative act of making them into daily life. We must do the work, however. Putting them on and wearing them won't change us. But the beads will assure us that the power is inside ourselves. If we are truly engaged in a spiritual practice—being present to what we are doing—we will understand that there are no mistakes, and that the experience is more important than the outcome. Seeing things as they are, rather than how we imagine them to be, will breathe change into our way of being in the world.

Working with prayer beads allows us to converse about spirituality. As we become more willing to share stories of ancestors, beliefs, and heirlooms, we also learn how to invite others into our lives. The possibilities for connection are endless. After the prayer-bead workshop that Eleanor presented in Bulgaria, one of the students wrote, "Well, I don't really know you, but I just want to say that I think that what you do is great. I'm not really a religious person, but actually I believe in something. One day, I guess, I'll find out what." Even in the places of not-knowing, we can find comfort and meaning in prayer beads.

Each of us has the power to make ourselves and our tools sacred. Too often we give our power away and say, "I have to read the book that the authority wrote." But you are the only authority of your own experience, and that's our fondest hope: that people come to see that their relationship to the Divine is the real authority in their lives.

Beads become prayer beads when making and using them is part of a meditation practice. If they are used as such, they remain prayer beads. If not, they're simply jewelry. But once you use them as prayer beads, you'll always remember that when you touch the beads: "Oh, when I got these, they were called 'prayer beads.'" In that moment, we can feel our feet on the floor and our grounding on the earth. If we continually bring small moments of silence into the lives we lead and stay in the present moment, our opportunities to notice spiritual connections will grow. Soon we will be able to sit with a cup of tea and really be present as we drink it. Soon our entire lives are a prayer.

Many people still think that meditation means sitting in a lotus position for twenty minutes with a quiet mind, but that's only one way to begin a meditation process. In meditation and contemplation, you bring yourself into the present moment as often as possible. You live life as it is happening, rather than let yourself get caught up in the past or the future. Many people designate a specific space for prayer, in which they learn how to make themselves present inside various activities, such as walking, running, writing, painting, eating, knitting, swimming, skiing. You cannot ski down a hill if you are not paying attention to where your feet are and where you are going. Find your own way of contacting stillness, learn to embrace that feeling of being grounded, and transfer it into other areas of your life.

A dramatic example of this involves a woman we know who converted to Catholicism but had never been exposed to the rosary. She was introduced to prayer beads after a car accident with her husband and five children. The car was hit head-on, and when she came to, her husband was gasping for breath and her children were covered with blood. She found herself reciting the "Our Father" over and over—she didn't know what else to do—and when she arrived at the hospital, a priest gave them all last rites. Someone handed her a rosary and she ended up holding it for days, running her fingers over the beads and using the "Hail Mary" as a mantra. All of them survived in spite of their severe injuries. When people in the hospital commented on her visible calm during the horrifying ordeal, she said that the beads gave her peace and grounded her.

In his book, *Praying by Hand,* M. Basil Pennington explores the way prayer beads make spiritual practice tangible.

> Fingering beads often helps our concentration. This is one of their greater benefits. While they occupy and integrate our external senses into our prayer, our mind is left freer to attend to its own level of reality. There are mysteries to be pondered and experiences to be had, moments of enlightenment and touches of the divine, while the beads and their accompanying formulas keep the lower faculties occupied. Even when the rational mind is occupied in conversation or some other simple task, beads can support the spirit in its course of prayer. Deliberately holding the beads can in itself be the prayer, especially when the mind seems unable to formulate any meaningful thoughts. The chain of beads can reach far beyond itself, bonding us with a higher power—with heaven itself. (4)

There are so many ways in which you can use your prayer beads for present-moment practice. What we offer below are only suggestions. We hope you will enjoy exploring the many ways in which the beads may assist you in discovering your own personal prayers.

✸ Beginning a New Day

Each morning when you wake, reach for your prayer beads, let the texture awake your fingers, and allow this vitality to permeate your entire body. Now you are ready to set your intentions for the day. These can include anything you would like to emphasize during your day: listening to people more carefully, telling the truth, being grateful for small things. Later, as you make your way through your day, touching the beads will return you to your initial intentions.

✸ Walking in the Present Moment

As you move from one place to another during the day, use these moments as a time to acknowledge the transition between tasks. Bring your beads into the palm of your hand, and as you feel their texture, let that be a reminder to feel your feet on the floor and take a breath—feeling both the inhalation and exhalation. Focus your mind on the physical activities of walking and breathing. Bring yourself into the present, and this focus will slow down the pace of your mind and heart.

Eleanor likes to use this practice when talking to someone. Appreciating the adage that we were given two ears and only one mouth for a reason, Eleanor uses her prayer beads as a tactile reminder to allow silence its place in her conversations.

✺ Grounding Practice

During important conversations or even thinking about things by ourselves, we can find ourselves getting caught up in "what was" and "what if." You can use your beads to ground you when you find yourself worrying about the past or the future. When things get difficult, take up your beads and allow their pleasing weight to bring you into the present moment. You will then be able to see more clearly into the current situation. By remaining grounded in the present, you will be more open to listening and accepting life as it is, rather than as you wish it to be.

✺ Ending the Day

When you are in bed and ready for sleep, pick up your beads and let their texture resonate in your body. As you rediscover each bead passing through your fingers, let yourself feel grateful for your day. It's also important to recognize the pain we might have caused or experienced. By acknowledging the truth of who we are, we can change and grow. As you approach sleep, breathe in and out with an awareness of your body. As you breathe in, focus on your toes, and on the exhalation, relax them. Continue breathing and moving up your entire body until you reach the top of your head. It's perfectly okay to fall asleep while you are traveling.

✸ *Gaining Strength from Your Roots*

You may make prayer beads that integrate family heirlooms and keepsakes. While all of these practices can be done using any and all prayer beads, this one is specifically designed to be done with family beads.

Hold the beads in your hands, and as you move through them, recall the particular energies and strengths of the person each amulet represents. Let the beads remind you that you are not alone, and that your ancestors are with you at all times.

One woman made prayer beads for her daughter using her grandmother's wedding ring, a cross the woman was given at her first Holy Communion at age seven, and additional beads with family significance. When her daughter is fearful—most often of being around a lot of people—she wears her beads and holds the end piece in her hand to ground herself so that she can remain in the crowd. The beads reassure her that her mother and her grandmother are with her, and that she will survive the anxious moment.

✸ *Special Passages*

It can be very meaningful to make a strand of prayer beads to commemorate special passages in our lives. For instance, you might want to make a strand of prayer beads to honor a journey that was important to you, using beads and symbols native to the area you traveled in and incorporating colors that remind you of that place. If you're a woman just beginning or ending menstruation, or if you've received a degree, launched a new business, or made any kind of big life change, you can honor it with prayer beads symbolic of this personal passage to help you carry your intentions for it forward.

✸ *Battling Addictions*

Addictions come in many forms, but usually two things are involved when engaged in them: a certain amount of time, and your hands. Whether you're trying to quit smoking, stop drinking, spend less, or eat more mindfully, creating prayer beads as a symbol of your intention can be a powerful aid. And one of the benefits is immediate: You can't engage in an addiction and make prayer beads at the same time!

Your prayer piece could help you visualize freedom from your addiction. For instance, someone who is trying to quit smoking might make a bracelet or handheld piece out of pink beads to represent clear lung tissue. A compulsive shopper might want to craft something out of gold-toned beads or coins to represent abundance already at hand. You might use alphabet beads to spell out an affirmation, or a rune charm that symbolizes freedom. Pick whatever elements speak most strongly and clearly to your desire to be free from your addiction. Keep your piece with you at all times and let it be a companion and comfort as you begin your recovery.

✹ Celebrating Achievements

Creating prayer beads that honor achievements can acknowledge the obstacles that you've conquered through faith, as well as give you a wonderful incentive to keep persevering toward a long-term goal. You can add beads to a prayer piece when you accomplish parts of a big task, which can look impossible in its totality. Trying to lose weight? You could add a progress bead to a string for every five pounds lost. Finally decided to write that novel? You could add a bead for every chapter you finish. When you've completed your goal, your prayer beads will testify to taking it "one day at a time"—and will be great encouragement as you pursue the next dream on your list!

✹ Honoring Your Dreams

Prayer beads can be created to honor your dreams, all kinds of dreams. If you have a particularly meaningful dream while sleeping with lots of rich images, you can continue working with that dream by creating prayer beads that represent the symbols given to you by your unconscious.

Similarly, prayer beads can be made to honor the waking dreams you have for your life. If you want to quit your job and become an artist, for example, you could create prayer beads with colorful components, perhaps adding amulets in the shape of painters' palettes or brushes.

You can also make prayer beads that reflect what you see as your life purpose. After composing her life-purpose statement, Maggie made a prayer-bead bracelet on a coiled wire, spelling out the words with the tiny black-and-white alphabet beads that hospitals once used for baby bracelets. Interspersing spacers between each word, she added amulets of personal significance to each end of the coil.

Like beads themselves, every person is unique, and each set of prayer beads will reflect that individuality. Perhaps that is the greatest gift of prayer beads: They teach us to trust ourselves, to integrate rather than segment ourselves, to create meaning for ourselves, and finally to align ourselves with the most powerful force in the universe—even if, like that Bulgarian student back in chapter 3, we're still living with questions about what exactly it is we believe in.

Making Prayer Beads for Others

Hanging in the Bead Museum in Glendale, Arizona, is this observation by the Tibetan Buddhist teacher Chagdud Tulku Rinpoche: that prayer beads, rosaries, and talismans are used in humanity's universal search and need to "engage in an act born of our longing to transcend the confines of self-reference." We can transcend self-reference when we make prayer beads as well. We can incorporate our prayers for someone into a piece with beads consciously chosen for him while we work. When we make prayer beads for someone far away, we are giving her the gift of our touch each time she fingers the beads.

✹ *Healing*

You may choose to make a set of prayer beads for someone injured or ill. As you put each bead on the string, offer your prayer for his healing. Presenting the beads is an opportunity to share your gift of prayer with another. She can either use the beads for prayer, or just be in the presence of your prayers.

Maggie made a prayer-bead bracelet for a dear friend facing surgery on her leg. She used blue and green stones to promote healing, added amulets with particular meaning to her friend, and included a Mexican healing charm called a *milagro,* in the shape of a leg. Her friend was moved to tears by the gift of the bracelet, knowing that it tangibly represented Maggie's love and prayers for her.

Maggie made a longer piece—one that could be worn around the neck, as well as around the wrist or held in the hand—for a friend battling breast cancer. Because her friend had mentioned how important Kuan Yin was to her, Maggie included an enameled representation of that Chinese goddess of compassion as the centerpiece of the necklace.

✴ Leave-Taking

When a dear friend from Australia was leaving the United States after completing her graduate work, Debra—a Northern California health educator—was extremely sad and wanted to do something to honor their friendship. Her friend gave her a bead—and that gave Debra, who had never done any beading before, an idea. "I started a necklace with that bead, and every time I missed her, I bought another bead and added it to the necklace," Debra remembers. "It was a way to embody the loss and create something beautiful from it." Since that time, Debra has continued to make prayer beads, using the same format she intuitively created for her very first necklace: beads that can be worn as a double strand, or as a long single strand. She continues to wear her first bead creation (see photo on page 80), which remains deeply significant to her: "I love wearing it because it really does bring my friend's presence so close to my heart."

AMY O'CONNELL

DEBRA'S BEADS TO HONOR HER AUSTRALIAN FRIEND

✸ Memorializing a Life

Another form of leave-taking is through death. When her beloved cat, Luna, was dying, Maggie made a strand of prayer beads for Luna that she knew would also serve to honor her pet's memory (see photo, page 81). Maggie chose colors that were found in Luna's fur coat—black, brown, cream—and added beads and charms that represented not only Luna's appearance, but also her spirit. The center piece is a tiger's-eye moon. When she is not wearing it, Maggie keeps the strand draped over Luna's picture and cherishes the memory of Luna's last night alive, when her precious kitty sat beside her on a blanket covering the couch, watching Maggie as she strung those beads.

MAGGIE'S BEADS TO HONOR HER CAT LUNA

❋ Weddings

To commemorate a wedding, gather beads and amulets from each side of the couple's family. Make a strand of each with a loop at one end; and when you have finished, put the two loops together to symbolize two families joining into one. The new couple can use this piece to help communication, to signal to the other partner that he or she has the floor and needs to speak without interruption. The piece's association with their wedding day will remind them of the importance of the vows they took.

You can also string marriage prayer beads during an engagement party or bridal shower, when the guests can bring a bead (or two, one for each member of the couple) representing a quality of marriage or their hopes for the couple. The completed prayer beads will always recall the community of friends and family encircling the new partnership.

Babies

For people about to enter the joyful and challenging world of parenthood, either through pregnancy or adoption, prayer beads can facilitate a wonderful present-moment practice during the long waiting period before the child arrives. Prayer beads can be made for the child during a baby shower; ask every guest to bring a bead that represents his or her hopes for the new arrival.

Prayer beads can also be made for women hoping to become pregnant, using symbols and amulets that signify fertility. Again, a group of family members or friends could collectively make a strand of fertility beads for the hopeful parent(s)-to-be, adding their prayers as they add their beads.

❈ Child-Custody Cases

A mother Eleanor met was suffering greatly, because her ex-husband had custody of her children. How could she let them know that she cared? How could she be with them when they were sad or happy, and wanted to share with their mom? Eleanor suggested that the woman make a special string of beads for each of her children, infusing each strand with her prayers and affection while she was stringing them. Adding on a special amulet that symbolized something personal between each child and herself, the woman gave these strands to each of her children, letting them know that the beads symbolized her love and caring. She told them that they could take the beads, hold on to them, and know that their mom's thoughts and prayers were present, even though she could not be with them in person. She also had the children choose beads and amulets to put together for her, so she could hold them near while they were away. Even prayer beads can't substitute for real contact, but it comforted both the mother and her children, and helped all of them to feel grace in the present moment.

❈ Those in Need of Housing

When Eleanor heard that Maggie and her husband had suddenly been given notice to move out of their rented house, she made a small handheld piece that included a red glass heart

ELEANOR WILEY

BEADS FOR MAGGIE'S HOUSE HUNT

bead and two silver charms, a small house and a key (see photo above), and sent it to Maggie with a card. Since Maggie was looking to find a place to live in the crowded and expensive San Francisco housing market, Eleanor knew that many emotions attended the housing search. "I couldn't change the situation," Eleanor says. "But I could let her know that my prayers were with her in a tangible way." Maggie looped the piece around her wrist and wore it every day, finding it very soothing when going through the stressful process of attending open houses and writing offers. Today, it hangs commemoratively in the hallway of the house that she and her husband ultimately bought.

✤ *Those Who Are Lonely*

Mildred is a ninety-five-year-old woman living in an assisted-living facility. When Eleanor asked her what she missed most, her answer was swift: "My family." Eleanor asked her if she would like family prayer beads, a reminder she could hold in her hands to say a quick prayer when she felt lonely for them. Oh, yes! was her reply. Eleanor sat with her and asked her to name all the people she would like to remember. Mildred not only named her immediate family, but also friends who had adopted her as a mother figure, as well as her husband, who had died many years before. As Eleanor chose the beads for each member of Mildred's circle of loved ones, she added a prayer for them. Since Mildred's vision is failing, Eleanor chose large, brightly colored beads that Mildred could both see well and feel. Each one was distinct and distinguishable just by the texture.

As Mildred's story illustrates, it is important to keep the special needs and concerns of others in mind when making prayer beads for them. And, of course, the most meaningful element you can include in the prayer beads that you make for others is your own prayer for their happiness and well-being.

Making Prayer Beads for Communities

Making personal prayer beads with other people in community is like the twenty-first-century equivalent of the quilting bee. If you get people together into this kind of circle, start with a discussion about prayer in general, and mention the fact that our whole lives can be prayer if we stay awake. Note too that there is no "right way" to pray, and that it's always good to trust our inner selves.

Often when people come together, they get so excited about the beads that they start worrying. They'll ask themselves, "Will I get the ones that I want? Should I stand back and let someone else have that one? Should I let people know what I want?" Observing the worry itself is a great spiritual exercise. Invite members of the group to notice their concerns when approaching the beads. Often a group situation like this can indicate the way we approach life in general. In a safe space such as a prayer-bead-making group, participants have the opportunity to listen to their self-talk and to their thoughts about others.

As people begin to choose the style and elements of the prayer beads they wish to make, they often defer to others, not wanting to appear selfish, or not trusting their own likes and dislikes. You'll see people wanting the workshop leader or the person sitting next to them to make their choices for them. But when they begin to trust themselves and their choices, they will probably find—as Eleanor and Maggie have—that some of the best work comes out of first making a technical mistake. That is what the beads can teach: trust yourself, trust the Divine, it's okay to make a mistake—and walk through the door that's open.

People often come to a workshop with a particular idea in mind, something they wish to work with. Quiet descends on the group, and as people start to string their beads, feelings arise. Beading provides the container and time to reflect, to discover, to quietly share with others in a safe and sacred place. When beading, we can open to both sorrow and joy. Each bead will reflect this understanding as it is placed on the string.

Though our completed pieces often look quite different from how we had first imagined them, usually we are surprised and delighted at how beautiful they are, and how perfectly they suit our original intention. When working with a group, it is nice to take the time to share the surprises that occur during this form of active contemplation.

We can learn so much from the smallest details of our beading experience. For instance, Eleanor always cuts more material than she needs because her arthritic fingers cannot deal with tiny bits and ends. We need to discover and accommodate our individual needs and limitations. For example, if you cannot see small holes, choose beads with larger holes. By learning to honor our strengths and difficulties as we create our prayer beads, we can become more compassionate when we are not beading—with ourselves and with others. Everyone works differently. Some approach things intuitively, others analytically. With prayer beads, as with life itself, any way you feel called to work is the right way.

Whether you make prayer beads in community with others or for a community of others, they can represent particular prayer concerns—such as women around the world, animals, or the environment. Find representations of those beings or that issue for which you are praying, and incorporate those symbols into your prayer beads. As with the prayer beads for special passages, these strands hold a more specifically focused intention. When using them, you become mindful not only of the present moment, but of your interconnectedness in the great web of life.

✸ Caregivers

Often residents who live in long-term care or rehabilitation facilities want to recognize the staff on special occasions, but they don't know how to do this without the opportunity, the money, and the mobility. A creative way around these limitations is to ask each resident for old beads or for a medallion or charm that can be donated to a community Gratitude Bowl. When a staff member has a birthday, baby, or other special passage, the residents can string together a strand of beads that represents the entire community. All residents become part of the gift of gratitude, and staff members get the acknowledgment they deserve. Each resident can add whatever prayers feel called for as the group puts the beads together. Residents can tell stories about where the beads or charms came from, and family members can contribute their own elements when they come to visit.

✸ Families

Eleanor made a prayer-bead piece to remind her to pray for her family (see photo, page 90). On it, she included the Sacred Wheel of Peace that she designed with her ex-husband, because of how it symbolizes reconciliation and working together. Explains Eleanor, "My family is very far apart. As a society we're so used to that, that I wonder if we even realize how distant we can be from each other. So I decided to make prayer beads for my family to help me remember to pray for them every morning and night."

Eleanor has a big family, so she cut her string 24 inches long, then folded it in half. She placed her Sacred Prayer Wheel on a loop at the end of the strand, and left two strands hanging down—one representing the men in her family and one representing the women, all of whom now range in age from sixty-five to eighty-one. Eleanor chose the color blue for the female side and green for the male side, stringing different beads and

ELEANOR'S FAMILY PRAYER BEADS

textures for each person. Eleanor represented her father on the end of the male strand with yellow, and her mother on the female side with red. "I take them with me to meditation," Eleanor says. "They go many places with me now—I wonder if they are enjoying the trip!"

Teachers

Making peace beads with her granddaughter's second-grade class, Eleanor noticed the children listening carefully as she talked about the Sacred Wheel and its symbols of various faith traditions. Each of the children identified the symbol that was part of his or her heritage. Like a little United Nations, all wanted to share their cultures and backgrounds with the others.

For their strands, Eleanor used simple cotton cord and beads with large holes that would string easily. Each child had the opportunity to make whatever he or she wanted. Eleanor asked the students to choose a special bead with their teacher in mind, representing something they were grateful for that happened during the year.

At the end of the session, the students got to talk about what they had done, and they were particularly excited about the beads they chose for their teacher. The children gave the beads to Eleanor, and she made prayer beads for the teacher that represented the children who had been in her care for that year.

When Eleanor explained there could be no mistakes because it was their personal piece, all the children became quiet and focused, even the boy who is so hyperactive that he has his own teacher's aide. His mother told Eleanor at the beginning of the next school year that he still works with his beads. A psychologist later suggested that beads could help overactive kids to remain still. How? Here's one practice: Have the children make their beads on a fairly long string. When they want to get up and move about the classroom, ask them to count their beads before they get up to move.

✺ Women and Children Around the World

At the Crones' Counsel—a gathering of women mostly over fifty, held yearly since 1993—a call went out for prayer beads to remember the women and children of the world. A basket of beads was put on the altar, and each woman was asked to take a bead home with her for use in a strand made in honor of all the women and children of the world. In making this string, the participants could extend the energy of the gathering to other women unable to attend. The single bead would begin the strand, to which other women in each Crone's home community would contribute beads. The energy and prayers of this one circle of women could then remember the larger group of women and children throughout the world.

The women were also asked to keep their own basket of beads in their homes, and to give other women visiting their homes a bead, so that those women could start their own strands.

If you'd like to try this kind of practice yourself, remember that beads can come from anywhere, including broken strands at a thrift store. Following the example of the Crones' Council, each time you get a group of women together, give a bead to the newcomers so that they can start their own strands of beads to pray for the women and children of the world. Invite them to keep a bead basket in their homes to share with those who visit them—beginning yet another circle of prayer!

Don't worry about how you string them, or on what you string them—remember that it is the prayer practice you are developing that counts, not the configuration of the beads. We can keep passing the beads on and praying to remember all the women and children of the world. When the women and the children of the world are protected, fed, and honored, then the boys and men of the world will also be whole.

✺ *Spiritual Leaders*

When Eleanor went to India in 1998 for The Way of Peace Retreat, she decided before she left to make interfaith prayer beads for Father Lawrence, the founder of the World Community for Christian Meditation, and for His Holiness the Dalai Lama. She made them out of *rudraksha* beads, the ones most often used for Buddhist malas; olive-wood beads from an old Catholic rosary; antique Muslim prayer beads from Afghanistan; and crystal beads from a rosary given to Eleanor by her mother in 1957. For amulets, Eleanor used a Benedictine cross that she had made in Bali for her Christian meditation community (the Hesed Community in Oakland, California) and a California-jade stone carved with the root mantra of the Tibetan Buddhist community.

Eleanor carried the beads with her to India, not knowing if she would have the opportunity to give them to the leaders or not, but for Eleanor, that did not make too much difference.

What made the difference was her prayer when she was making them. When she arrived, she asked the logistics person if he could see to it that Father Lawrence and His Holiness got their beads, but he told her to just hold on to them for a while. Eleanor did, but decided that she wanted everyone to give this gift, so she left them on the end of the dinner table and asked the group members to pick them up, hold them, and offer a prayer for each of these wonderful men. As it turns out, Eleanor got the opportunity to present the beads to the two spiritual leaders during the closing ceremony—and she was so over-whelmed by the experience that she can't remember their response!

Animals

Prayer beads can be made for any population or issue of partic-ular importance to your heart. Maggie made a prayer piece for the animals of the world, which too often are ignored, used, or even abused by human beings. Her prayer strand has mammals, reptiles, fish, and birds: a cast of a netsuke frog, an amethyst dol-phin, a jasper coyote, a jade snake, a mother-of-pearl bird. Touching the different shapes and textures of each animal rep-resentation in prayer evokes awareness of the special and unique—and sadly, in many cases endangered—creatures we share the planet with.

⚘ Earth and the Environment

To create prayer beads that honor the planet Earth and our environment, try gathering recycled beads and amulets, and stringing them together in a way pleasing to you. Let them remind you to conserve the resources of the world; let them bring prayers of protection for the earth into your conscious mind.

Debra, who made the beads commemorating her Australian friend mentioned in chapter 4, had another idea for planet Earth prayer beads. After the events of September 11, 2001, Debra needed to create something beautiful, so she made prayer beads out of clear emerald and spring-green stones (see photo, page 96). Says Debra, "I used green because it is a color of rebirth and regeneration. I used an infinity symbol and Celtic and goddess symbols. To me, the piece represents the 'greening' of the world—and also my hope for a beautiful future."

⚘ Rescue Workers

One month after September 11, 2001, Eleanor met with the faculty of the George Washington University Health and Spirituality program. Focus and quiet had not been easy for many in this group, especially for a young man who, on his first day as an ambulance crew intern, was assigned to the airplane crash at the Pentagon. He faced total devastation and death. Instead of working to save people, he spent the day putting bodies into

AMY O'CONNELL

DEBRA'S BEADS FOR "GREENING" THE WORLD

body bags. Coping with his vivid memories was so very difficult; he was distracted and unable to concentrate. He came to the prayer-bead class because he could not think of anything else to do. He hoped that maybe doing something reverent would help him feel better. After the beading part of the workshop he said that focusing on putting the string through the beads gave his mind an opportunity to rest—and that this was the first time during that past month that his mind had been able to rest. He allowed himself to sink into the beads and string, offering his distraction to the Divine. Having something to hold on to helped to bring him into the present and away from the horror of the past. With the beads he could not have the answers. All he had to do was stay in the present. For him and other rescue workers, prayer beads offer a physicality that can ground them even in very stressful moments.

✳ *Political Leaders*

In this time of great global fragility, it is perhaps more important than ever to pray for political leaders. Eleanor made a prayer piece using red, white, and blue beads to represent the United States flag, a peace symbol, and the Sacred Wheel to honor all people on the earth and to remind her of our interconnectedness. She keeps this small handheld piece in her car, and each time she gets in or out of the vehicle, the piece reminds her to say a special prayer for the president and other national leaders, asking that they may be guided toward peace while making their decisions.

✳ *Peace*

A young man named Bertan, who took a workshop with Eleanor in Romania, relates his experience of making prayer beads and giving them to his grandmother.

There were three bombs in my part of town in a sequence a couple of days ago—one just two hundred meters away and the other two four hundred meters away from where I live. It is horrible 'cause now I am staying with my gran because she is scared to be alone, so I promised that I'll stay with her all the time. It does get lonely sometimes because I don't go out at all, and I sometimes can't tell all my problems to my gran—she just doesn't understand my age—but it has been very educating for me to be with her because she is very intelligent and has taught me to never speak before thinking over what I want to say. . . . She is a very sad woman (many things happened to her) and worries about many things and always thinks that she is ill—so I make her forget about the bad things by amusing her with my humor.

So I am not able to go out and enjoy nightlife in Skopje. It's strange how people can hate me when they don't even know me—you know, there is one thing I learned from the seminar and that's that one can always enjoy every moment of life; it's just a question of how you perceive life. Ever since I came back from Romania to Macedonia where I live now, I have never felt bored because I look for the best in things and believe that life is short and CARPE DIEM of course.

Guess what? I gave my gran a string of beads and I

was telling her what they mean to me and to a whole group of people around the world—and that if I should be out sometimes, that she could always keep the beads and imagine me in the beads, touching my chin and cheeks as she always does in real life. Now she never loses sight of them—you know, it's the psychological character of the beads that really soothes her soul. Now she thinks more of herself and the love around her rather than the hate and the killings.

I just wish I could do more to help this situation but I can't, 'cause no one is willing to hear out the ideas of a twenty-year-old Turkish-Albanian, which is not very welcome here in Macedonia. But I'm strong and I'll manage and I believe—actually I know—that everything will be okay and that one day I'll look back and laugh at the stupidity but also shed tears for all those innocent people who are dying daily for nothing.

✵ Remembrance

Eleanor was in Central Illinois on September 11, 2001, to see her brother, a recent stroke victim whom she hadn't seen for over a year. Feeling confused, Eleanor wasn't sure what to do so far away from home. When she heard the news from the East Coast and Pennsylvania, she was glued to the radio, but decided she had to keep doing what she does. "I was in the middle of

AMY O'CONNELL

ELEANOR'S BEADS FOR REMEMBRANCE

antique country, so off I went to the antique stores—I talked about the bombings with people I did not know, I talked about the Sacred Wheel of Peace."

As Eleanor wandered through the dusty symbols of America's past, she came across the brittle body of an old china doll that looked as though she had been buried for a long time. For Eleanor, this little piece of porcelain immediately became a symbol of that dreadful day, a symbol of the innocents and innocence we lost. Eleanor made this piece part of a special strand of beads (see photo above) that remind her of her own mortality and the mortality of our world. Even more important, her beads remind her that she—and all of us—must bring ourselves into a place of peace, and to share that place with others. In the end, all prayer beads are about peace—coming to this place within ourselves so that we can be at peace with others.

Prayers for Contemplation with Beads

As you will discover working with beads, there is a natural rhythm in touching each bead in a strand while reciting a prayer. While every faith path that incorporates prayer beads has its own traditional prayers, any prayer can be used in conjunction with prayer beads. Experiment with these that follow, or write your own. Each prayer offered here is simply a place to begin.

> Wherever I go—only Thou!
> Wherever I stand—only Thou!
> Just Thou, again Thou! Always Thou!
> Thou, Thou, Thou!
> When things are good, Thou!
> When things are bad, Thou!
> Thou, Thou, Thou!
>
> *—Hasidic song*

With your feet I walk
I walk with your limbs
I carry forth your body
For me your mind thinks
Your voice speaks for me
Beauty is before me
And beauty is behind me
Above and below me hovers the beautiful
I am surrounded by it
I am immersed in it
In my youth I am aware of it
And in old age I shall walk quietly
The beautiful trail.

—Navajo prayer

Look to this day,
For it is life,
The very life of life.
In its brief course lie all
The realities and verities of existence,
The bliss of growth,
The splendor of action,
The glory of power—

For yesterday is but a dream,
And tomorrow is only a vision,
But today, well lived,
Makes every yesterday a dream of happiness
And every tomorrow a vision of hope.

    —*Sanskrit proverb*

Christ has no body now on earth but ours;
Ours are the only hands with which he can do his
  work,
Ours are the only feet with which he can go about
  the world,
Ours are the only eyes through which his
  compassion
    can shine forth upon a troubled world.
Christ has no body on earth now but ours.

—Adapted from a prayer of St. Teresa of Avila

Thou my mother, and my father thou
Thou my friend, and my teacher thou
Thou my wisdom, and my riches thou
Thou art all to me, O God of all Gods.

—*Ramanuja Indian prayer*

Today I remember that I am One with all.
Earth, ground and nurture me
And connect me to the Divine Mother
Who loves and protects all her children.
Divine Mother, send your blessing of comfort and
    protection to . . .

> *[using the prayer beads, mention names of persons,*
> *groups, projects, or nations]*

Air, breathe life into me
And connect me to the Great Spirit
Who inspires all and dwells in all.
Great Spirit, send your blessing of inspiration and
    serenity to . . .

Fire, enflame me with passion
And connect me to the God/Goddess of
    Compassion
Who equally embraces and supports all.
God/Goddess of Compassion, send your blessing
    of mercy and joy to . . .

Water, cleanse and empower me
And connect me to the Source of Life
Who flows in all and through all.
Source of Life, send your blessing of refreshment
   and abundance to . . .

Today I am grateful that I am One with All.

> —*Adapted from a traditional Buddhist*
> *loving-kindness meditation by Barbara Rose Billings*

Love is such a special thing
When you love a person
It is so hard to leave them.
You realize how much joy and love you spent
  with them.
But to love someone is to be with them
And when the time has come to leave, there is
  nothing to say but "I love you."
But I know that when I get scared, there is
  nothing to say.
I must just hope and pray that you are fine.
The time I spent with you is all I must look
  back to,
But there is a time when you must leave and
  that time
Can come anytime.

—*Jennifer Tattersall (written when she was 11)*

Lord, make me an instrument of your peace.
Where there is hatred, let me sow love,
Where there is injury, pardon;
Where there is doubt, faith;
Where there is despair, hope;
Where there is darkness, light;
And where there is sadness, joy.

O, Divine Master, grant that I may not so much
Seek to be consoled as to console,
To be understood as to understand,
To be loved, as to love.

For it is in giving that we receive,
It is in pardoning that we are pardoned,
And it is in dying that we are born to eternal life.

—St. Francis of Assisi

From the cowardice that dare not face new truth
From the laziness that is contented with half truth
From the arrogance that thinks it knows all truth,
Good Lord, deliver me.

—Kenyan prayer

O God, of peace and love,
Companion in solitude,
Protector in exile,
You inhabit the shadows of our communities
Show us the way to stand against injustice
To protect and nurture life, to live nonviolently.

Help us to embrace simplicity,
To be mindful of the value of all things,
To care tenderly for others.

Teach us to conserve
And preserve the natural gifts of this world
Help us to take time and to be present
To one another.

Increase among us the spirit of tolerance
And good will.
Bring us to the quiet still place of healing
And transform our souls into a reflection
Of Your love and compassion. Amen.

—*Anonymous*

Let me seek you in my desire,
Let me desire you in my seeking.
Let me find you by loving you
Let me love you when I find you.

—*St. Anselm*

O God, give me, I pray Thee,
light on my right hand
and light on my left hand
and light above me
and light beneath me.
Lord, increase light within me
and give me light
and illuminate me.

—*Ascribed to Mohammed*

'Tis the gift to be simple,
'Tis the gift to be free,
'Tis the gift to come down
Where we ought to be—
And when we find ourselves
In the place just right,
'Twill be in the valley
Of love and delight.
When true simplicity is gained,
To bow and to bend
We shan't be asham'd,
To turn, turn, will be our delight,
Till by turning, turning
We come round right.

          —Shaker hymn

O Lord, grant me to greet
The coming day in peace.
Help me in all things
To rely upon thy holy will.
In every hour of the day
Reveal thy will to me.
Bless my dealings
With all who surround me.
Teach me to treat all that comes to me
Throughout the day with peace of soul,
And with firm conviction that
Thy will governs all.
In all my deeds and words
Guide my thoughts and feelings.
In unforeseen events
Let me not forget that all are sent by thee.
Teach me to act firmly and wisely,
Without embittering and embarrassing others.
Give me strength to bear the fatigue
Of the coming day with all that it shall bring.
Direct my will, teach me to pray,
Pray thou thyself in me. Amen.

—Eastern Orthodox prayer

More hearts are open
Uniting in compassion
Touched by loving spirits
Aware of God's light.

It is about America
And it's so much bigger, too.
For we are just one nation
That is a part of the world.

We are awakened to our interdependence
We are called to care.
For in this place of beauty
We have a vision to share.

Our responsibility is peace
How we contribute is the question
May we seek the answers
Creating harmony and giving love to all today.

           —Tami Briggs (written one month after 9/11/01)

God grant me the serenity to accept the things
   I cannot change;
Courage to change the things I can;
and wisdom to know the difference.
Living one day at a time;
Enjoying one moment at a time;
Accepting hardships as the pathway to peace;
Taking this sinful world as it is, not as I would
   have it;
Trusting that you will make all things right if
   I surrender to your will;
That I may be reasonably happy in this life
And supremely happy with you forever in the next.

   —*Attributed to Reinhold Niebuhr*

If anyone has hurt me or harmed me knowingly or
   unknowingly in thought, word, or deed, I freely
   forgive them.
And I too ask forgiveness if I have hurt anyone or
   harmed anyone knowingly or unknowingly in
   thought, word, or deed.

May I be happy
May I be peaceful
May I be free

May my friends be happy
May my friends be peaceful
May my friends be free

May my enemies be happy
May my enemies be peaceful
May my enemies be free

May all things be happy
May all things be peaceful
May all things be free.
                    —*Buddhist prayer*

Not Christian or Jew or Muslim, not Hindu,
Buddhist, Sufi, or Zen. Not any religion

or cultural system. I am not from the East
or the West, not out of the ocean or up

from the ground, not natural or ethereal, not
composed of elements at all. I do not exist,

am not an entity in this world or the next,
did not descend from Adam and Eve or any

origin story. My place is placeless, a trace
of the traceless. Neither body or soul.

I belong to the beloved, have seen the two
worlds as one and that one call to and know,

first, last, outer, inner, only that
breath breathing human being.

—*Rumi (translated by Coleman Barks)*

Resources for Further Exploration

A PLACE TO BEGIN

Books

⊛ *Beads and Jewelry*

Aikman, Z. Susanne. *A Primer: The Art of Native American Beadwork.* Denver: Morning Flower Press, 1980.

Bigham, Elizabeth. *African Beads.* New York: The Metropolitan Museum of Art and Simon & Schuster, 1999.

Coles, Janet, and Robert Budwig. *Beads.* New York: Simon & Schuster Editions, 1997.

———. *The Book of Beads.* New York: Simon & Schuster, 1990.

Dubin, Lois Sherr. *The History of Beads.* New York: Harry N. Abrams, Inc., 1987.

Erikson, Joan Mowat. *The Universal Bead.* New York: W.W. Norton & Co., 1993.

Harris, Elizabeth. *Introduction to Beads from the West African Trade.* Vol. 5. Carmel, CA: Picard African Imports, 1989.

Jargstorf, Sibylle. *Ethnic Jewelry from Africa, Europe and Asia.* Atglen, PA: Schiffer Publishing, Ltd., 2000.

Larsen, Michael. *The Worry Bead Book.* New York: St. Martin's Press, 1989.

Liu, Robert K. *Collectible Beads.* Vista, CA: Ornament, Inc., 1995.

Melody. *Love Is in the Earth: A Kaleidoscope of Crystals Update.* Wheat Ridge, CO: Earth-Love Publishing House, 1995.

Newman, Harold. *An Illustrated Dictionary of Jewelry.* New York: Thames and Hudson, Inc., 1981.

Tomalin, Stefany. *The Bead Jewelry Book.* Lincolnwood, IL: Contemporary Books, 1998.

Symbolism

Arrien, Angeles. *Signs of Life.* Sonoma, CA: Arcus Publishing Co., 1992.

Bruce-Mitford, Miranda. *The Illustrated Book of Signs & Symbols.* New York: DK Publishing, Inc., 1996.

Cooper, J. C. *An Illustrated Encyclopedia of Traditional Symbols.* New York: Thames and Hudson, Inc., 1998.

Gettig, Lynda Jessen. *The History of the Cross in Religious & Political Symbolism.* Wickenburg, AZ: Rainbow Hogan Museum of the Cross, 1989.

Hitchcock, Helyn. *Helping Yourself with Numerology.* West Nyack, NY: Parker Publishing Company, Inc., 1972.

Kunz, George Frederick. *The Magic of Jewels and Charms.* Mineola, NY: Dover Publications, Inc., 1997.

Matthews, Boris, trans. *The Herder Symbol Dictionary.* Wilmette, IL: Chiron Publications, 1991.

Prayer Practices and Spirituality

Arettam, Joanna. *Dharma Beads.* Boston: Journey Editions, 2000.

Bowes, Susan. *Life Magic.* New York: Simon & Schuster Editions, 1999.

De Montfort, St. Louis Mary. *The Secret of the Rosary.* Bay Shore, NY: Montfort Fathers Publications, 1954.

Gill, Jean. *Pray As You Can.* Notre Dame, IN: Ave Maria Press, 1989.

Hastings, Joanna. *The Rosary: Prayer for All Seasons.* Collegeville, MN: The Liturgical Press, 1993.

Hutchinson, Gloria. *Praying the Rosary.* Cincinnati: St. Anthony Messenger Press, 1991.

Hutson, Joan. *Praying with Sacred Beads.* Liguori, MO: Liguori Publications, 2000.

Judith, Anodea. *Wheels of Life: A User's Guide to the Chakra System.* St. Paul, MN: Llewellyn Publications, 1989.

Laurie, Erynn Rowan. *A Circle of Stones.* Chicago: Eschaton Productions, Inc., 1998.

Linn, Denise. *Altars.* New York: The Ballantine Publishing Group, 1999.

Mascetti, Manuela Dunn, and Priya Hemenway. *Prayer Beads.* New York: Viking Compass/Penguin Putnam, Inc., 2001.

Meyer, Marvin and Richard Smith, eds. *Ancient Christian Magic.* New York: HarperSanFrancisco, 1994.

Oman, Maggie, *Prayers for Healing.* Berkeley: Conari Press, 1997.

Oman Shannon, Maggie. *The Way We Pray.* Berkeley, CA: Conari Press, 2001.

Pennington, M. Basil. *Praying by Hand.* New York:
    HarperSanFrancisco, 1991.
Schiller, David, ed. *The Little Book of Prayers.* New York:
    Workman Publishing, 1996.
Streep, Peg. *Altars Made Easy.* New York: HarperSanFrancisco,
    1997.
"Structure and Surface: Beads in Contemporary American
    Art." Exhibition catalogue. Sheboygan, WI: John Michael
    Kohler Arts Center, 1990.
Weber, Christin Lore. *Circle of Mysteries.* St. Paul, MN: Yes
    International Publishers, 1995.

Magazines

Beads: The Journal of the Society of Bead Researchers
56489 El Dorado Drive
Yucca Valley, CA 92284-4230

Beadwork (published bimonthly)
201 E. Fourth Street
Loveland, CO 80537
970-669-7672
E-mail: beadwork@interweave.com
www.interweave.com

Lapidary Journal
www.lapidaryjournal.com
Good for reference and finding supplies and shows.

Ornament: The Art of Personal Adornment
Subscriptions: 800-888-8950
E-mail: ornament@cts.com

Miscellaneous Interest

The New Story
501 Bella Vista Way
San Francisco, CA 94127
Phone: 415-333-6424
Inner-Life Line: 415-451-RENEW (7363)
www.thenewstory.com
Spiritual direction and workshops offered by Maggie Oman Shannon.

Recipe for Rose Beads

1 cup salt
1 cup rose petals, firmly packed
½ cup water
oil paint (optional)

1. Heat salt and petals, mashing together. Stir in water and paint for desired color, or leave natural for a brown bead.

2. Reheat very low over an asbestos pad, stirring constantly until smooth.

3. Roll out to ¼-inch thickness. Cut and roll beads in the palm of your hand to desired shape until they are smooth.

4. String beads on florist's wire or waxed string fastened to a needle. Let beads dry in a dark place, moving them occasionally to keep from sticking.

5. When dry, make prayer beads as desired.

Museums

The Bead Museum
5754 W. Glenn Drive
Glendale, AZ 95301
623-930-7395

The Bead Museum in DC
400 Seventh Street NW
Washington, D.C. 20004
202-624-4500

Rainbow Hogan Museum of the Cross
P.O. Box 2413
Wickenburg, AZ 85358
602-684-5745

Organizations

 Beads

The Bead Society
P.O. Box 241874
Los Angeles, CA 90024

The Center for Bead Research
4 Essex Street
Lake Placid, NY 12946

The Center for the Study of Beadwork
P.O. Box 13719
Portland, OR 97213

Northern California Bead Society
P.O. Box 22128
Oakland, CA 94623
510-869-2723
www.norcalbead.org
Monthly programs held third Tuesday of each month.

The Society of Bead Researchers
P.O. Box 7304
Eugene, OR 97401

✾ *Spirituality*

Parliament of the World's Religions
70 East Lake Street, Suite 205
Chicago, IL 60601
312-629-2990
www.cpwr.org

World Community for Christian Meditation
www.wccm.org

✸ *Retail Outlets*

Bead Castle
2049 University Avenue
Berkeley, CA 94704
510-848-5653
Wonderful antique beads and contemporary beads.

The Bead Store
417 Castro Street
San Francisco, CA 94114
415-861-7332
A small shop with a big emphasis on ethnic jewelry and religious iconography.

Contemporary Prayer Beads
1402 Santa Clara Avenue
Alameda, CA 94501
510-865-1349
E-mail: prayerbdzs@aol.com
www.prayerbdzs.com
The work of Eleanor Wiley: Sacred Wheel of Peace and one-of-a-kind prayer beads.

Leekan Designs
93 Mercer Street
New York, NY 10012
212-226-7226
E-mail: info@leekandesigns.com
www.leekandesigns.com

Supplies

Fire Mountain Gems
28195 Redwood Highway
Cave Junction, OR 97523
To order: 800-355-2137 (24 hours)
Customer Service: 800-423-2319; fax: 800-292-3473
www.firemountaingems.com
Catalog that carries everything you need to get started—tools and beads. Very helpful to customers.

International Gem and Jewelry Show, Inc.
www.intergem.net
Gem show presented throughout the United States; sells both wholesale and retail.

Rio Grande
www.riogrande.com
Supplies and beads.

Shipwreck Beads
2500 Mottman Road SW
Olympia, WA 98521
800-950-4232
www.shipwreck-beads.com

Soft Flex Wire
P.O. Box 60
Sonoma, CA 95476
707-938-3539
E-mail: info@softflexcompany.com
www.softflexwire.com
Most flexible, strong wire around.

Websites

www.rosaryshop.com
Many supplies and good links available here.

www.craftsbyjanetlynn.com
Short articles on prayer beads and some useful links.

www.fourgates.com/malause.asp
An interesting article called "Care and Use of Your Mala."

www.rings-things.com/bead-res.htm
A number of bead resources, some of which are already listed here.

www.guidetobeadwork.com/localstores/
A directory of more than twelve hundred bead stores worldwide.

www.beadshows.com/ibs/articles/prayer.html
More on the history of prayer beads.

http://members.ols.net/~michael/PrayerBeads.html
More on the history of prayer beads.

A PLACE TO BEGIN